Arizona Rules of Evidence 2018

Table of Contents

Prefatory Comment to 2012 Amendments

<u>Currentness</u>

The 2012 amendments to the Arizona Rules of Evidence make three different kinds of changes: (1) the Arizona rules have generally been restyled so that they correspond to the Federal Rules of Evidence as restyled. These "restyling" changes are not meant to change the admissibility of evidence; (2) in several instances, the Arizona rules have also been amended to "conform" to the federal rules, and these changes may alter the way in which evidence is admitted (see, e.g., Rule 702); and (3) in some instances, the Arizona rules either retain language that is distinct from the federal rules (see, e.g., Rule 404), or deliberately depart from the language of the federal rules (see, e.g., Rule 412).

The Court has generally adopted the federal rules as restyled, with the following exceptions: Rule 103(d) (Fundamental Error); Rule 302; Rule 404 (Character and Other Acts Evidence); Rule 408(a)(2) (Criminal Use Exception); Rule 611(b) (Scope of Cross-Examination); Rule 706(c) (Compensation for Expert Testimony); Rule 801(d)(1)(A) (Prior Inconsistent Statements as Non-Hearsay); Rule 803(25) (Former testimony (non-criminal action or proceeding)); and Rule 804(b)(1) (Former Testimony in a Criminal Case). The restyling is intended to make the rules more easily understood and to make style and terminology consistent throughout the rules and with the restyled Federal Rules. Restyling changes are intended to be stylistic only, and not intended to change any ruling on the admissibility of evidence.

The Court has adopted conforming changes to Rule 103 (Rulings on Evidence); Rule 201 (Judicial Notice); Rule 301 (Presumptions); Rule 407 (Subsequent Remedial Measures); Rule 410 (Plea Discussions); Rules 412-415; Rule 606 (Juror's Competency as a Witness); Rule 608 (Character Evidence); Rule 609 (Impeachment by Criminal Conviction); Rule 611 (Mode of Presenting Evidence); Rule 615 (Excluding Witnesses); Rule 701 (Opinion Testimony by Lay Witnesses); Rule 702 (Testimony by Expert Witnesses); Rule 704(b) (Opinion on an Ultimate Issue--Exception); Rule 706 (Court Appointed Experts); Rule 801(d)(2) (Definitions That Apply to This Article; Exclusions from Hearsay); Rule 803(6)(A), (6)(D) and (24) (Hearsay Exceptions Regardless of Unavailability); Rule 804 (b)(1), (b)(3) and (b)(7) (Hearsay Exceptions When Declarant Unavailable); and Rule 807 (Residual Exception).

Conforming changes that are not merely restyling, as well as deliberate departures from the language of the federal rules, are noted at the outset of the comment to the corresponding Arizona rule.

Where the language of an Arizona rule parallels that of a federal rule, federal court decisions interpreting the federal rule are persuasive but not binding with respect to interpreting the Arizona rule.

Credits

Added Sept. 8, 2011, effective Jan. 1, 2012. Amended Aug. 30, 2012, effective Jan. 1, 2013.

17A Pt. 1 A. R. S. Rules of Evid., Prefatory Comment, AZ ST REV Prefatory Comment

Article I. General Provisions

Rule 101. Scope; Definitions

<u>Currentness</u>
(a) Scope. These rules apply to proceedings in courts in the State of Arizona. The specific courts and proceedings to which the rules apply, along with exceptions, are set out in Rule 1101.
(b) Definitions. In these rules:
(1) "civil case" means a civil action or proceeding;
(2) "criminal case" includes a criminal proceeding;
(3) "public office" includes a public agency;
(4) "record" includes a memorandum, report, or data compilation;
(5) a "rule prescribed by the Supreme Court" means a rule adopted by the Arizona Supreme Court; and
(6) a reference to any kind of written material or any other medium includes electronically stored information.

Credits
Amended Sept. 8, 2011, effective Jan. 1, 2012.

Editors' Notes

COMMENT TO 2012 AMENDMENT
The language of Rule 101 has been amended, and definitions have been added, to conform to the federal restyling of the Evidence Rules to make them more easily understood and to make style and terminology consistent throughout the rules. These changes are intended to be stylistic only. There is no intent to change any result in any ruling on evidence admissibility.

COMMENT TO ORIGINAL 1977 RULE
These rules apply in all courts, record and nonrecord, in Arizona.

HISTORICAL NOTE

Source:
Federal Rules of Evidence, Rule 101.
17A Pt. 1 A. R. S. Rules of Evid., Rule 101, AZ ST REV Rule 101
Current with amendments received through 11/1/17

Rule 102. Purpose

<u>Currentness</u>

These rules should be construed so as to administer every proceeding fairly, eliminate unjustifiable expense and delay, and promote the development of evidence law, to the end of ascertaining the truth and securing a just determination.

Credits
Amended Sept. 8, 2011, effective Jan. 1, 2012.

Editors' Notes
COMMENT TO 2012 AMENDMENT
The language of Rule 102 has been amended to conform to the federal restyling of the Evidence Rules to make them more easily understood and to make style and terminology consistent throughout the rules. These changes are intended to be stylistic only. There is no intent to change any result in any ruling on evidence admissibility.

HISTORICAL NOTE
Source:
Federal Rules of Evidence, Rule 102.
17A Pt. 1 A. R. S. Rules of Evid., Rule 102, AZ ST REV Rule 102
Current with amendments received through 11/1/17

Rule 103. Rulings on Evidence

Currentness

(a) Preserving a Claim of Error. A party may claim error in a ruling to admit or exclude evidence only if the error affects a substantial right of the party and:

(1) if the ruling admits evidence, a party, on the record:

(A) timely objects or moves to strike; and

(B) states the specific ground, unless it was apparent from the context; or

(2) if the ruling excludes evidence, a party informs the court of its substance by an offer of proof, unless the substance was apparent from the context.

(b) Not Needing to Renew an Objection or Offer of Proof. Once the court rules definitively on the record--either before or at trial--a party need not renew an objection or offer of proof to preserve a claim of error for appeal.

(c) Court's Statement About the Ruling; Directing an Offer of Proof. The court may make any statement about the character or form of the evidence, the objection made, and the ruling. The court may direct that an offer of proof be made in question-and-answer form.

(d) Preventing the Jury from Hearing Inadmissible Evidence. To the extent practicable, the court must conduct a jury trial so that inadmissible evidence is not suggested to the jury by any means.

(e) Taking Notice of Fundamental Error. A court may take notice of an error affecting a fundamental right, even if the claim of error was not properly preserved.

Credits
Amended Sept. 8, 2011, effective Jan. 1, 2012.

Editors' Notes
COMMENT TO 2012 AMENDMENT
Subsection (b) has been added to conform to Federal Rule of Evidence 103(b).

Additionally, the language of Rule 103 has been amended to conform to the federal restyling of the Evidence Rules to make them more easily understood and to make style and terminology consistent throughout the rules. These changes are intended to be stylistic only. There is no intent in the restyling to change any result in any ruling on evidence admissibility.

The substance of subsection (e) (formerly subsection (d)), which refers to "fundamental error," has not been changed to conform to the federal rule, which refers to "plain error," because Arizona and federal courts have long used different terminology in this regard.

HISTORICAL NOTE

Source:

Fed.Rules Civ.Proc., Rule 43(c), 28 U.S.C.A.Code 1939, § 25-923.
Federal Rules of Evidence, Rule 103 (modified).
17A Pt. 1 A. R. S. Rules of Evid., Rule 103, AZ ST REV Rule 103
Current with amendments received through 11/1/17

Rule 104. Preliminary Questions

Currentness

(a) In General. The court must decide any preliminary question about whether a witness is qualified, a privilege exists, or evidence is admissible. In so deciding, the court is not bound by evidence rules, except those on privilege.

(b) Relevance That Depends on a Fact. When the relevance of evidence depends on whether a fact exists, proof must be introduced sufficient to support a finding that the fact does exist. The court may admit the proposed evidence on the condition that the proof be introduced later.

(c) Conducting a Hearing So That the Jury Cannot Hear It. The court must conduct any hearing on a preliminary question so that the jury cannot hear it if:

(1) the hearing involves the admissibility of a confession;

(2) a defendant in a criminal case is a witness and so requests; or

(3) justice so requires.

(d) Cross-Examining a Defendant in a Criminal Case. By testifying on a preliminary question, a defendant in a criminal case does not become subject to cross-examination on other issues in the case.

(e) Evidence Relevant to Weight and Credibility. This rule does not limit a party's right to introduce before the jury evidence that is relevant to the weight or credibility of other evidence.

Credits

Amended Oct. 19, 1988, effective Nov. 1, 1988; Sept. 8, 2011, effective Jan. 1, 2012.

Editors' Notes

COMMENT TO 2012 AMENDMENT

The language of Rule 104 has been amended to conform to the federal restyling of the Evidence Rules to make them more easily understood and to make style and terminology consistent throughout the rules. These changes are intended to be stylistic only. There is no intent to change any result in any ruling on evidence admissibility.

HISTORICAL NOTE

Source:
Federal Rules of Evidence, Rule 104.
17A Pt. 1 A. R. S. Rules of Evid., Rule 104, AZ ST REV Rule 104
Current with amendments received through 11/1/17

Rule 105. Limiting Evidence That Is Not Admissible Against Other Parties or for Other Purposes

Currentness

If the court admits evidence that is admissible against a party or for a purpose--but not against another party or for another purpose--the court, on timely request, must restrict the evidence to its proper scope and instruct the jury accordingly.

Credits

Amended Sept. 8, 2011, effective Jan. 1, 2012.

Editors' Notes

COMMENT TO 2012 AMENDMENT

The language of Rule 105 has been amended to conform to the federal restyling of the Evidence Rules to make them more easily understood and to make style and terminology consistent throughout the rules. These changes are intended to be stylistic only. There is no intent to change any result in any ruling on evidence admissibility.

HISTORICAL NOTE

Source:
Federal Rules of Evidence, Rule 105.
17A Pt. 1 A. R. S. Rules of Evid., Rule 105, AZ ST REV Rule 105
Current with amendments received through 11/1/17

Rule 106. Remainder of or Related Writings or Recorded Statements

Currentness

If a party introduces all or part of a writing or recorded statement, an adverse party may require the introduction, at that time, of any other part--or any other writing or recorded statement--that in fairness ought to be considered at the same time.

Credits

Amended Oct. 19, 1988, effective Nov. 1, 1988; Sept. 8, 2011, effective Jan. 1, 2012.

Editors' Notes

COMMENT TO 2012 AMENDMENT

The language of Rule 106 has been amended to conform to the federal restyling of the Evidence Rules to make them more easily understood and to make style and terminology consistent throughout the rules. These changes are intended to be stylistic only. There is no intent to change any result in any ruling on evidence admissibility.

HISTORICAL NOTE

Source:
Federal Rules of Evidence, Rule 106.
17A Pt. 1 A. R. S. Rules of Evid., Rule 106, AZ ST REV Rule 106

Article II. Judicial Notice

Rule 201. Judicial Notice of Adjudicative Facts

<u>Currentness</u>

(a) Scope. This rule governs judicial notice of an adjudicative fact only, not a legislative fact.

(b) Kinds of Facts That May Be Judicially Noticed. The court may judicially notice a fact that is not subject to reasonable dispute because it:

(1) is generally known within the trial court's territorial jurisdiction; or

(2) can be accurately and readily determined from sources whose accuracy cannot reasonably be questioned.

(c) Taking Notice. The court:

(1) may take judicial notice on its own; or

(2) must take judicial notice if a party requests it and the court is supplied with the necessary information.

(d) Timing. The court may take judicial notice at any stage of the proceeding.

(e) Opportunity to Be Heard. On timely request, a party is entitled to be heard on the propriety of taking judicial notice and the nature of the fact to be noticed. If the court takes judicial notice before notifying a party, the party, on request, is still entitled to be heard.

(f) Instructing the Jury. In a civil case, the court must instruct the jury to accept the noticed fact as conclusive. In a criminal case, the court must instruct the jury that it may or may not accept the noticed fact as conclusive.

Credits

Amended Sept. 8, 2011, effective Jan. 1, 2012.

Editors' Notes

COMMENT TO 2012 AMENDMENT

The last sentence of subsection (f) (formerly subsection (g)) has been added to conform to Federal Rule of Evidence 201(f), as restyled.

Additionally, the language of Rule 201 has been amended to conform to the federal restyling of the Evidence Rules to make them more easily understood and to make style and terminology consistent throughout the rules. These changes are intended to be stylistic only. There is no intent in the restyling to change any result in any ruling on evidence admissibility.

HISTORICAL NOTE

Source:

Federal Rules of Evidence, Rule 201, (modified).

Civ.Code 1913, §§ 1916, 1946.

Rev.Code 1928, § 4453.
Code 1939, § 23-304.
Rules Civ.Proc., former Rules 44(o), 44(p).
17A Pt. 1 A. R. S. Rules of Evid., Rule 201, AZ ST REV Rule 201
Current with amendments received through 11/1/17

Article III. Presumptions in Civil Cases

Rule 301. Presumptions in Civil Cases Generally

In a civil case, unless a statute or these rules provide otherwise, the party against whom a presumption is directed has the burden of producing evidence to rebut the presumption. But this rule does not shift the burden of persuasion, which remains on the party who had it originally.

Credits

Amended Sept. 8, 2011, effective Jan. 1, 2012.

Editors' Notes

COMMENT TO 2012 AMENDMENT

The language of this rule has been added to conform to Federal Rule of Evidence 301, as restyled.

17A Pt. 1 A. R. S. Rules of Evid., Rule 301, AZ ST REV Rule 301
Current with amendments received through 11/1/17

Rule 302. Applying State Law to Presumptions in Civil Cases

Currentness
<Not adopted.>

Editors' Notes

COMMENT TO 2012 AMENDMENT

Federal Rule of Evidence 302 has not been adopted because it is inapplicable to state court proceedings.

COMMENT TO ORIGINAL 1977 RULE

Federal Rule of Evidence 302 was not adopted because of the non-adoption of Rule 301. No other purpose was intended.

17A Pt. 1 A. R. S. Rules of Evid., Rule 302, AZ ST REV Rule 302
Current with amendments received through 11/1/17

Article IV. Relevancy and Its Limits

Rule 401. Test for Relevant Evidence

Currentness

Evidence is relevant if:

(a) it has any tendency to make a fact more or less probable than it would be without the evidence; and

(b) the fact is of consequence in determining the action.

Credits

Amended Sept. 8, 2011, effective Jan. 1, 2012.

Editors' Notes

COMMENT TO 2012 AMENDMENT

The language of Rule 401 has been amended to conform to the federal restyling of the Evidence Rules to make them more easily understood and to make style and terminology consistent throughout the rules. These changes are intended to be stylistic only. There is no intent to change any result in any ruling on evidence admissibility.

HISTORICAL NOTE

Source:

Federal Rules of Evidence, Rule 401.

17A Pt. 1 A. R. S. Rules of Evid., Rule 401, AZ ST REV Rule 401

Current with amendments received through 11/1/17

Rule 402. General Admissibility of Relevant Evidence

Currentness

Relevant evidence is admissible unless any of the following provides otherwise:

• the United States or Arizona Constitution;

• an applicable statute;

• these rules; or

• other rules prescribed by the Supreme Court.

Irrelevant evidence is not admissible.

Credits

Amended Sept. 8, 2011, effective Jan. 1, 2012.

Editors' Notes

COMMENT TO 2012 AMENDMENT

The language of Rule 402 has been amended to conform to the federal restyling of the Evidence Rules to make them more easily understood and to make style and terminology consistent throughout the rules. These changes are intended to be stylistic only. There is no intent to change any result in any ruling on evidence admissibility.

HISTORICAL NOTE

Source:

Federal Rules of Evidence, Rule 402, (modified).

17A Pt. 1 A. R. S. Rules of Evid., Rule 402, AZ ST REV Rule 402

Current with amendments received through 11/1/17

Rule 403. Excluding Relevant Evidence for Prejudice, Confusion, Waste of Time, or Other Reasons

Currentness

The court may exclude relevant evidence if its probative value is substantially outweighed by a danger of one or more of the following: unfair prejudice, confusing the issues, misleading the jury, undue delay, wasting time, or needlessly presenting cumulative evidence.

Credits

Amended Sept. 8, 2011, effective Jan. 1, 2012.

Editors' Notes

COMMENT TO 2012 AMENDMENT

The language of Rule 403 has been amended to conform to the federal restyling of the Evidence Rules to make them more easily understood and to make style and terminology consistent throughout the rules. These changes are intended to be stylistic only. There is no intent to change any result in any ruling on evidence admissibility.

HISTORICAL NOTE

Source:

Federal Rules of Evidence, Rule 403.

17A Pt. 1 A. R. S. Rules of Evid., Rule 403, AZ ST REV Rule 403

Current with amendments received through 11/1/17

Rule 404. Character Evidence not Admissible to Prove Conduct; Exceptions; Other Crimes

Currentness

(a) Character evidence generally. Evidence of a person's character or a trait of character is not admissible for the purpose of proving action in conformity therewith on a particular occasion, except:

(1) *Character of accused or civil defendant.* Evidence of a pertinent trait of character offered by an accused, or by the prosecution to rebut the same, or evidence of the aberrant sexual propensity of the accused or a civil defendant pursuant to Rule 404(c);

(2) *Character of victim.* Evidence of a pertinent trait of character of the victim of the crime offered by an accused, or by the prosecution to rebut the same, or evidence of a character trait of peacefulness of the victim offered by the prosecution in a homicide case to rebut evidence that the victim was the first aggressor;

(3) *Character of witness.* Evidence of the character of a witness, as provided in Rules 607, 608, and 609.

(b) Other crimes, wrongs, or acts. Except as provided in Rule 404(c) evidence of other crimes, wrongs, or acts is not admissible to prove the character of a person in order to show action in conformity therewith. It may, however, be admissible for other purposes, such as proof of motive, opportunity, intent, preparation, plan, knowledge, identity, or absence of mistake or accident.

(c) Character evidence in sexual misconduct cases

In a criminal case in which a defendant is charged with having committed a sexual offense, or a civil case in which a claim is predicated on a party's alleged commission of a sexual offense, evidence of other crimes, wrongs, or acts may be admitted by the court if relevant to show that the defendant had a character trait giving rise to an aberrant sexual propensity to commit the offense charged. In such a case, evidence to rebut the proof of other crimes, wrongs, or acts, or an inference therefrom, may also be admitted.

(1) In all such cases, the court shall admit evidence of the other act only if it first finds each of the following:

(A) The evidence is sufficient to permit the trier of fact to find that the defendant committed the other act.

(B) The commission of the other act provides a reasonable basis to infer that the defendant had a character trait giving rise to an aberrant sexual propensity to commit the crime charged.

(C) The evidentiary value of proof of the other act is not substantially outweighed by danger of unfair prejudice, confusion of issues, or other factors mentioned in Rule 403. In making that determination under Rule 403 the court shall also take into consideration the following factors, among others:

(i) remoteness of the other act;

(ii) similarity or dissimilarity of the other act;

(iii) the strength of the evidence that defendant committed the other act;

(iv) frequency of the other acts;

(v) surrounding circumstances;

(vi) relevant intervening events;

(vii) other similarities or differences;

(viii) other relevant factors.

(D) The court shall make specific findings with respect to each of (A), (B), and (C) of Rule 404(c)(1).

(2) In all cases in which evidence of another act is admitted pursuant to this subsection, the court shall instruct the jury as to the proper use of such evidence.

(3) In all criminal cases in which the state intends to offer evidence of other acts pursuant to this subdivision of Rule 404, the state shall make disclosure to the defendant as to such acts as required by Rule 15.1, Rules of Criminal Procedure, no later than 45 days prior to the final trial setting or at such later time as the court may allow for good cause. The defendant shall make disclosure as to rebuttal evidence pertaining to such acts as required by Rule 15.2, no later than 20 days after receipt of the state's disclosure or at such other time as the court may allow for good cause. In all civil cases in which a party intends to offer evidence of other acts pursuant to this subdivision of Rule 404, the parties shall make disclosure as required by Rule 26.1, Rules of Civil Procedure, no later than 60 days prior to trial, or at such later time as the court may allow for good cause shown.

(4) As used in this subsection of Rule 404, the term "sexual offense" is as defined in A.R.S. Sec. 13-1420(C) and, in addition, includes any offense of first-degree murder

pursuant to A.R.S. Sec. 13-1105(A)(2) of which the predicate felony is sexual conduct with a minor under Sec. 13-1405, sexual assault under Sec. 13-1406, or molestation of a child under Sec. 13-1410.

Credits

Amended Oct. 19, 1988, effective Nov. 1, 1988; Aug. 19, 1997, effective Dec. 1, 1997; Sept. 27, 2005, effective Dec. 1, 2005.

Editors' Notes

COMMENT TO 2012 AMENDMENT

The language of Rule 404 has not been changed in any manner. [Text of comment eff. Jan. 1, 2012.]

COMMENT TO 1997 AMENDMENT

Subsection (c) of Rule 404 is intended to codify and supply an analytical framework for the application of the rule created by case law in *State v. Treadaway,* 116 Ariz. 163, 568 P.2d 1061 (1977), and *State v. McFarlin,* 110 Ariz. 225, 517 P.2d 87 (1973). The rule announced in *Treadaway* and *McFarlin* and here codified is an exception to the common-law rule forbidding the use of evidence of other acts for the purpose of showing character or propensity.

Subsection (1)(B) of Rule 404(c) is intended to modify the *Treadaway* rule by permitting the court to admit evidence of remote or dissimilar other acts providing there is a "reasonable" basis, by way of expert testimony or otherwise, to support relevancy, i.e., that the commission of the other act permits an inference that defendant had an aberrant sexual propensity that makes it more probable that he or she committed the sexual offense charged. The *Treadaway* requirement that there be expert testimony in all cases of remote or dissimilar acts is hereby eliminated.

The present codification of the rule permits admission of evidence of the other act either on the basis of similarity or closeness in time, supporting expert testimony, or other reasonable basis that will support such an inference. To be admissible in a criminal case, the relevant prior bad act must be shown to have been committed by the defendant by clear and convincing evidence. *State v. Terrazas*, 189 Ariz. 580, 944 P.2d 1194 (1997).

Notwithstanding the language in *Treadaway,* the rule does not contemplate any bright line test of remoteness or similarity, which are solely factors to be considered under subsection (1)(c) of Rule 404(c). A medical or other expert who is testifying pursuant to Rule 404(c) is not required to state a diagnostic conclusion concerning any aberrant sexual propensity of the defendant so long as his or her testimony assists the trier of fact and there is other evidence which satisfies the requirements of subsection (1)(B). Subsection (1)(C) of the rule requires the court to make a Rule 403 analysis in all cases. The rule also requires the court in all cases to instruct the jury on the proper use of any other act evidence that is admitted. At a minimum, the court should instruct the jury that the admission of other acts does not lessen the prosecution's burden to prove the defendant's guilt beyond a reasonable doubt, and that the jury may not convict the defendant simply because it finds that he committed the other act or had a character trait that predisposed him to commit the crime charged.

COMMENT TO ORIGINAL 1977 RULE

State v. Superior Court, 113 Ariz. 22, 545 P.2d 946 (1976) is consistent with and interpretative of Rule 404(a)(2).

APPLICATION

<Applicable to cases pending on and after that date, except civil cases as to which the final trial date is set to occur between December 1, 1997 and February 1, 1998 and criminal cases as to which the final trial date is set to occur between December 1, 1997 and January 15, 1998.>

HISTORICAL NOTE

Source:

Federal Rules of Evidence, Rule 404.

17A Pt. 1 A. R. S. Rules of Evid., Rule 404, AZ ST REV Rule 404

Current with amendments received through 11/1/17

Rule 405. Methods of Proving Character

Currentness

(a) By Reputation or Opinion. When evidence of a person's character or character trait is admissible, it may be proved by testimony about the person's reputation or by testimony in the form of an opinion. On cross-examination of the character witness, the court may allow an inquiry into relevant specific instances of the person's conduct.

(b) By Specific Instances of Conduct. When a person's character or character trait is an essential element of a charge, claim, or defense, or pursuant to Rule 404(c), the character or trait may also be proved by relevant specific instances of the person's conduct.

Credits

Amended Oct. 19, 1988, effective Nov. 1, 1988; Aug. 19, 1997, effective Dec. 1, 1997; Sept. 8, 2011, effective Jan. 1, 2012.

Editors' Notes

COMMENT TO 2012 AMENDMENT

The language of Rule 405 has been amended to conform to the federal restyling of the Evidence Rules to make them more easily understood and to make style and terminology consistent throughout the rules. These changes are intended to be stylistic only. There is no intent to change any result in any ruling on evidence admissibility.

APPLICATION

Applicable to cases pending on and after that date, except civil cases as to which the final trial date is set to occur between December 1, 1997 and February 1, 1998 and criminal cases as to which the final trial date is set to occur between December 1, 1997 and January 15, 1998.

HISTORICAL NOTE

Source:

Federal Rules of Evidence, Rule 405.

Fed.Rules Civ.Proc., Rule 43(b), 28 U.S.C.A. Code 1939, § 21-922.

Rule Civ.Proc., former Rule 43(g).

17A Pt. 1 A. R. S. Rules of Evid., Rule 405, AZ ST REV Rule 405

Current with amendments received through 11/1/17

Rule 406. Habit; Routine Practice

Currentness

Evidence of a person's habit or an organization's routine practice may be admitted to prove that on a particular occasion the person or organization acted in accordance with the habit or routine practice. The court may admit this evidence regardless of whether it is corroborated or whether there was an eyewitness.

Credits

Amended Sept. 8, 2011, effective Jan. 1, 2012.

Editors' Notes

COMMENT TO 2012 AMENDMENT

The language of Rule 406 has been amended to conform to the federal restyling of the Evidence Rules to make them more easily understood and to make style and terminology consistent throughout the rules. These changes are intended to be stylistic only. There is no intent to change any result in any ruling on evidence admissibility.

HISTORICAL NOTE

Source:

Federal Rules of Evidence, Rule 406.

17A Pt. 1 A. R. S. Rules of Evid., Rule 406, AZ ST REV Rule 406

Current with amendments received through 11/1/17

Rule 407. Subsequent Remedial Measures

Currentness

When measures are taken that would have made an earlier injury or harm less likely to occur, evidence of the subsequent measures is not admissible to prove:

• negligence;

• culpable conduct;

• a defect in a product or its design; or

• a need for a warning or instruction.

But the court may admit this evidence for another purpose, such as impeachment or--if disputed--proving ownership, control, or the feasibility of precautionary measures.

Credits

Amended Sept. 8, 2011, effective Jan. 1, 2012.

Editors' Notes

COMMENT TO 2012 AMENDMENT

This rule has been amended to conform to Federal Rule of Evidence 407 in order to provide greater clarity regarding the applicable scope of the rule.

Additionally, the language of Rule 407 has been amended to conform to the federal restyling of the Evidence Rules to make them more easily understood and to make style and terminology consistent throughout the rules. These changes are intended to be stylistic only. There is no intent in the restyling to change any result in any ruling on evidence admissibility.

Rule 407 previously provided that evidence was not excluded if offered for a purpose not explicitly prohibited by the rule. To improve the language of the rule, it now provides that the court may admit evidence if offered for a permissible purpose. There is no intent to change the process for admitting evidence covered by the rule. It remains the case that if offered for an impermissible purpose, it must be excluded, and if offered for a purpose not barred by the rule, its admissibility remains governed by the general principles of Rules 402, 403, 801, etc.

HISTORICAL NOTE

Source:

Federal Rules of Evidence, Rule 407.

17A Pt. 1 A. R. S. Rules of Evid., Rule 407, AZ ST REV Rule 407

Current with amendments received through 11/1/17

Rule 408. Compromise Offers and Negotiations

<u>Currentness</u>

(a) Prohibited Uses. Evidence of the following is not admissible--on behalf of any party--either to prove or disprove the validity or amount of a disputed claim or to impeach by a prior inconsistent statement or a contradiction:

(1) furnishing, promising, or offering--or accepting, promising to accept, or offering to accept--a valuable consideration in compromising or attempting to compromise the claim; and

(2) conduct or a statement made during compromise negotiations about the claim.

(b) Exceptions. The court may admit this evidence for another purpose, such as proving a witness's bias or prejudice, negating a contention of undue delay, or proving an effort to obstruct a criminal investigation or prosecution.

Credits

Amended Sept. 3, 2009, effective Jan. 1, 2010; Sept. 8, 2011, effective Jan. 1, 2012.

Editors' Notes

COMMENT TO 2012 AMENDMENT

The 2012 amendment does not include any substantive changes and does not include the "criminal use exception" in Federal Rule of Evidence 408(a)(2).

Otherwise, the language of Rule 408 has been amended to conform to the federal restyling of the Evidence Rules to make them more easily understood and to make style and terminology consistent throughout the rules. These changes are intended to be stylistic only. There is no intent to change any result in any ruling on evidence admissibility.

Rule 408 previously provided that evidence was not excluded if offered for a purpose not explicitly prohibited by the rule. To improve the language of the rule, it now provides that the court may admit evidence if offered for a permissible purpose. There is no intent to change the process for admitting evidence covered by the rule. It remains the case that if offered for an impermissible purpose, it must be excluded, and if offered for a purpose not barred by the rule, its admissibility remains governed by the general principles of Rules 402, 403, 801, etc.

The reference to "liability" has been deleted on the ground that the deletion makes the rule flow better and easier to read, and because "liability" is covered by the broader term "validity." Courts have not made substantive decisions on the basis of any distinction between validity and liability. No change in current practice or in the coverage of the rule is intended.

HISTORICAL NOTE

Source:

Federal Rules of Evidence, Rule 408.

17A Pt. 1 A. R. S. Rules of Evid., Rule 408, AZ ST REV Rule 408

Current with amendments received through 11/1/17

Rule 409. Offers to Pay Medical and Similar Expenses

Currentness

Evidence of furnishing, promising to pay, or offering to pay medical, hospital, or similar expenses resulting from an injury is not admissible to prove liability for the injury.

Credits

Amended Sept. 8, 2011, effective Jan. 1, 2012.

Editors' Notes

COMMENT TO 2012 AMENDMENT

The language of Rule 409 has been amended to conform to the federal restyling of the Evidence Rules to make them more easily understood and to make style and terminology consistent throughout the rules. These changes are intended to be stylistic only. There is no intent to change any result in any ruling on evidence admissibility.

HISTORICAL NOTE

Source:

Federal Rules of Evidence, Rule 409.

17A Pt. 1 A. R. S. Rules of Evid., Rule 409, AZ ST REV Rule 409

Current with amendments received through 11/1/17

Rule 410. Pleas, Plea Discussions and Related Statements

Currentness

(a) Prohibited Uses. Except as otherwise provided by statute, in a civil or criminal case, or administrative proceeding, evidence of the following is not admissible against the defendant who made the plea or participated in the plea discussions:

(1) a guilty plea that was later withdrawn;

(2) a nolo contendere or no contest plea;

(3) a statement made during a proceeding on either of those pleas under Arizona Rule of Criminal Procedure 17.4 or a comparable federal procedure; or

(4) a statement made during plea discussions with an attorney for the prosecuting authority if the discussions did not result in a guilty plea or they resulted in a later-withdrawn guilty plea.

(b) Exceptions. The court may admit a statement described in Rule 410(a)(3) or (4):

(1) in any proceeding in which another statement made during the same plea or plea discussions has been introduced, if in fairness the statements ought to be considered together; or

(2) in a criminal proceeding for perjury or false statement, if the defendant made the statement under oath, on the record, and with counsel present.

Credits

Amended Sept. 8, 2011, effective Jan. 1, 2012.

Editors' Notes

COMMENT TO 2012 AMENDMENT

This rule has been amended to conform to Federal Rule of Evidence 410, including the addition of subdivision (b)(2) and the Arizona-specific provision in subdivision (a)(3). Additionally, the language of Rule 410 has been amended to conform to the federal restyling of the Evidence Rules to make them more easily understood and to make style and terminology consistent throughout the rules. These changes are intended to be stylistic only. There is no intent in the restyling to change any result in any ruling on evidence admissibility.

Arizona Rule of Criminal Procedure 17.4(f) has also been amended to conform to its federal counterpart, Federal Rule of Criminal Procedure 11(f).

HISTORICAL NOTE

Source:

Federal Rules of Evidence, Rule 410, as modified, consistent with Rule 17.4, Arizona Rules of Criminal Procedure.

17A Pt. 1 A. R. S. Rules of Evid., Rule 410, AZ ST REV Rule 410

Current with amendments received through 11/1/17

Rule 411. Liability Insurance

Currentness

Evidence that a person was or was not insured against liability is not admissible to prove whether the person acted negligently or otherwise wrongfully. But the court may admit this evidence for another purpose, such as proving a witness's bias or prejudice or proving agency, ownership, or control.

Credits

Amended Oct. 19, 1988, effective Nov. 1, 1988; Sept. 8, 2011, effective Jan. 1, 2012.

Editors' Notes

COMMENT TO 2012 AMENDMENT

The language of Rule 411 has been amended to conform to the federal restyling of the Evidence Rules to make them more easily understood and to make style and terminology consistent throughout the rules. These changes are intended to be stylistic only. There is no intent to change any result in any ruling on evidence admissibility. Rule 411 previously provided that evidence was not excluded if offered for a purpose not explicitly prohibited by the rule. To improve the language of the rule, it now provides that the court may admit evidence if offered for a permissible purpose. There is no intent to change the process for admitting evidence covered by the rule. It remains the case that if offered for an impermissible purpose, it must be excluded, and if offered for a purpose not barred by the rule, its admissibility remains governed by the general principles of Rules 402, 403, 801, etc.

HISTORICAL NOTE

Source:

Federal Rules of Evidence, Rule 411.

17A Pt. 1 A. R. S. Rules of Evid., Rule 411, AZ ST REV Rule 411

Current with amendments received through 11/1/17

Rule 412. Sex-Offense Cases: The Victim's Sexual Behavior or Predisposition

Currentness

<Not adopted.>

Editors' Notes

COMMENT TO 2012 AMENDMENT

Federal Rule of Evidence 412 has not been adopted. *See* A.R.S. § 13-1421 (Evidence relating to victim's chastity; pretrial hearing).

17A Pt. 1 A. R. S. Rules of Evid., Rule 412, AZ ST REV Rule 412

Current with amendments received through 11/1/17

Rule 413. Similar Crimes in Sexual-Assault Cases

Currentness

<Not adopted.>

Editors' Notes

COMMENT TO 2012 AMENDMENT

Federal Rule of Evidence 413 has not been adopted. *See* Arizona Rule of Evidence 404(c).

17A Pt. 1 A. R. S. Rules of Evid., Rule 413, AZ ST REV Rule 413

Current with amendments received through 11/1/17

Rule 414. Similar Crimes in Child-Molestation Cases

Currentness

<Not adopted.>

Editors' Notes

COMMENT TO 2012 AMENDMENT

Federal Rule of Evidence 414 has not been adopted. *See* Arizona Rule of Evidence 404(c).

17A Pt. 1 A. R. S. Rules of Evid., Rule 414, AZ ST REV Rule 414

Current with amendments received through 11/1/17

Rule 415. Similar Acts in Civil Cases Involving Sexual Assault or Child Molestation

Currentness

<Not adopted.>

Editors' Notes

COMMENT TO 2012 AMENDMENT

Federal Rule of Evidence 415 has not been adopted. *See* Arizona Rule of Evidence 404(c).

17A Pt. 1 A. R. S. Rules of Evid., Rule 415, AZ ST REV Rule 415

Current with amendments received through 11/1/17

Article V. Privileges

Rule 501. Privilege in General

Currentness

The common law--as interpreted by Arizona courts in the light of reason and experience--governs a claim of privilege unless any of the following provides otherwise:
• the United States or Arizona Constitution;
• an applicable statute; or
• rules prescribed by the Supreme Court.

Credits

Amended Sept. 8, 2011, effective Jan. 1, 2012.

Editors' Notes

COMMENT TO 2012 AMENDMENT

The language of Rule 501 has been amended to conform to the federal restyling of the Evidence Rules to make them more easily understood and to make style and terminology consistent throughout the rules. These changes are intended to be stylistic only. There is no intent to change any result in any ruling on evidence admissibility.

HISTORICAL NOTE

Source:

Federal Rules of Evidence, Rule 501, (modified).

17A Pt. 1 A. R. S. Rules of Evid., Rule 501, AZ ST REV Rule 501

Current with amendments received through 11/1/17

Rule 502. Attorney-Client Privilege and Work Product; Limitations on Waiver

The following provisions apply, in the circumstances set out, to disclosure of a communication or information covered by the attorney-client privilege or work-product protection.

(a) Disclosure made in an Arizona proceeding; scope of a waiver.

When the disclosure is made in an Arizona proceeding and waives the attorney-client privilege or work-product protection, the waiver extends to an undisclosed communication or information in an Arizona proceeding only if:

(1) the waiver is intentional;

(2) the disclosed and undisclosed communications or information concern the same subject matter; and

(3) they ought in fairness to be considered together.

(b) Inadvertent disclosure.

When made in an Arizona proceeding, the disclosure does not operate as a waiver in an Arizona proceeding if:

(1) the disclosure is inadvertent;

(2) the holder of the privilege or protection took reasonable steps to prevent disclosure; and

(3) the holder promptly took reasonable steps to rectify the error, including (if applicable) following Arizona Rule of Civil Procedure 26(b)(6)(B).

(c) Disclosure made in a proceeding in federal court or another state.

When the disclosure is made in a proceeding in federal court or another state and is not the subject of a court order concerning waiver, the disclosure does not operate as a waiver in an Arizona proceeding if the disclosure:

(1) would not be a waiver under this rule if it had been made in an Arizona proceeding; or

(2) is not a waiver under the law governing the federal or state proceeding where the disclosure occurred.

(d) Controlling effect of a court order.

An Arizona court may order that the privilege or protection is not waived by disclosure connected with the litigation pending before the court--in which event the disclosure is also not a waiver in any other proceeding.

(e) Controlling effect of a party agreement.

An agreement on the effect of disclosure in an Arizona proceeding is binding only on the parties to the agreement, unless it is incorporated into a court order.

(f) Definitions.

In this rule:

(1) "attorney-client privilege" means the protection that applicable law provides for confidential attorney-client communications; and

(2) "work-product protection" means the protection that applicable law provides for tangible material (or its intangible equivalent) prepared in anticipation of litigation or for trial.

Credits

Added Sept. 3, 2009, effective Jan. 1, 2010. Amended Sept. 8, 2011, effective Jan. 1, 2012; Sept. 2, 2016, effective Jan. 1, 2017.

17A Pt. 1 A. R. S. Rules of Evid., Rule 502, AZ ST REV Rule 502

Article VI.☐ Witnesses

Rule 601. Competency to Testify in General

<u>Currentness</u>

Every person is competent to be a witness unless these rules or an applicable statute provides otherwise.

Credits

Amended Sept. 8, 2011, effective Jan. 1, 2012.

Editors' Notes

COMMENT TO 2012 AMENDMENT

The language of Rule 601 has been amended to conform to the federal restyling of the Evidence Rules to make them more easily understood and to make style and terminology consistent throughout the rules. These changes are intended to be stylistic only. There is no intent to change any result in any ruling on evidence admissibility.

HISTORICAL NOTE

Source:

Federal Rules of Evidence, Rule 601, (modified).

17A Pt. 1 A. R. S. Rules of Evid., Rule 601, AZ ST REV Rule 601

Current with amendments received through 11/1/17

Rule 602. Need for Personal Knowledge

<u>Currentness</u>

A witness may testify to a matter only if evidence is introduced sufficient to support a finding that the witness has personal knowledge of the matter. Evidence to prove personal knowledge may consist of the witness's own testimony. This rule does not apply to a witness's expert testimony under Rule 703.

Credits

Amended Oct. 19, 1988, effective Nov. 1, 1988; Sept. 8, 2011, effective Jan. 1, 2012.

Editors' Notes

COMMENT TO 2012 AMENDMENT

The language of Rule 602 has been amended to conform to the federal restyling of the Evidence Rules to make them more easily understood and to make style and terminology consistent throughout the rules. These changes are intended to be stylistic only. There is no intent to change any result in any ruling on evidence admissibility.

HISTORICAL NOTE

Source:

Federal Rules of Evidence, Rule 602.

17A Pt. 1 A. R. S. Rules of Evid., Rule 602, AZ ST REV Rule 602

Current with amendments received through 11/1/17

Rule 603. Oath or Affirmation to Testify Truthfully

Currentness

Before testifying, a witness must give an oath or affirmation to testify truthfully. It must be in a form designed to impress that duty on the witness's conscience.

Credits

Amended Oct. 19, 1988, effective Nov. 1, 1988; Sept. 8, 2011, effective Jan. 1, 2012.

Editors' Notes

COMMENT TO 2012 AMENDMENT

The language of Rule 603 has been amended to conform to the federal restyling of the Evidence Rules to make them more easily understood and to make style and terminology consistent throughout the rules. These changes are intended to be stylistic only. There is no intent to change any result in any ruling on evidence admissibility.

HISTORICAL NOTE

Source:

Federal Rules of Evidence, Rule 603.

17A Pt. 1 A. R. S. Rules of Evid., Rule 603, AZ ST REV Rule 603

Current with amendments received through 11/1/17

Rule 604. Interpreters

Currentness

An interpreter must be qualified and must give an oath or affirmation to make a true translation.

Credits

Amended Oct. 19, 1988, effective Nov. 1, 1988; Sept. 8, 2011, effective Jan. 1, 2012.

Editors' Notes

COMMENT TO 2012 AMENDMENT

The language of Rule 604 has been amended to conform to the federal restyling of the Evidence Rules to make them more easily understood and to make style and terminology consistent throughout the rules. These changes are intended to be stylistic only. There is no intent to change any result in any ruling on evidence admissibility.

HISTORICAL NOTE

Source:

Federal Rules of Evidence, Rule 604.

17A Pt. 1 A. R. S. Rules of Evid., Rule 604, AZ ST REV Rule 604

Current with amendments received through 11/1/17

Rule 605. Judge's Competency as a Witness

Currentness

The judge presiding at trial may not testify as a witness at the trial. A party need not object to preserve the issue.

Credits
Amended Sept. 8, 2011, effective Jan. 1, 2012.

Editors' Notes
COMMENT TO 2012 AMENDMENT
The language of Rule 605 has been amended to conform to the federal restyling of the Evidence Rules to make them more easily understood and to make style and terminology consistent throughout the rules. These changes are intended to be stylistic only. There is no intent to change any result in any ruling on evidence admissibility.
HISTORICAL NOTE
Source:
Federal Rules of Evidence, Rule 605.
17A Pt. 1 A. R. S. Rules of Evid., Rule 605, AZ ST REV Rule 605
Current with amendments received through 11/1/17

Rule 606. Juror's Competency as a Witness

<u>Currentness</u>

(a) At the Trial. A juror may not testify as a witness before the other jurors at the trial. If a juror is called to testify, the court must give a party an opportunity to object outside the jury's presence.

(b) During an Inquiry into the Validity of a Verdict in a Civil Case.

(1) *Prohibited Testimony or Other Evidence.* During an inquiry into the validity of a verdict in a civil case, a juror may not testify about any statement made or incident that occurred during the jury's deliberations; the effect of anything on that juror's or another juror's vote; or any juror's mental processes concerning the verdict or indictment. The court may not receive a juror's affidavit or evidence of a juror's statement on these matters.

(2) *Exceptions.* A juror may testify about whether:

(A) extraneous prejudicial information was improperly brought to the jury's attention;

(B) an outside influence was improperly brought to bear on any juror; or

(C) a mistake was made in entering the verdict on the verdict form.

Credits
Amended Oct. 19, 1988, effective Nov. 1, 1988; Sept. 8, 2011, effective Jan. 1, 2012.

Editors' Notes
COMMENT TO 2012 AMENDMENT
This rule has been amended to conform to Federal Rule of Evidence 606, including the addition of subdivision (b)(2)(C). However, subsection (b) has not been applied to criminal cases, as is done in Federal Rule of Evidence 606(b), because the matter is covered by Arizona Rule of Criminal Procedure 24.1(d).

Additionally, the language of Rule 606 has been amended to conform to the federal restyling of the Evidence Rules to make them more easily understood and to make style and terminology consistent throughout the rules. These changes are intended to be stylistic only. There is no intent in the restyling to change any result in any ruling on evidence admissibility.

HISTORICAL NOTE
Source:
Federal Rules of Evidence, Rule 606, (modified).
17A Pt. 1 A. R. S. Rules of Evid., Rule 606, AZ ST REV Rule 606
Current with amendments received through 11/1/17

Rule 607. Who May Impeach a Witness

Currentness

Any party, including the party that called the witness, may attack the witness's credibility.

Credits
Amended Oct. 19, 1988, effective Nov. 1, 1988; Sept. 8, 2011, effective Jan. 1, 2012.

Editors' Notes
COMMENT TO 2012 AMENDMENT
The language of Rule 607 has been amended to conform to the federal restyling of the Evidence Rules to make them more easily understood and to make style and terminology consistent throughout the rules. These changes are intended to be stylistic only. There is no intent to change any result in any ruling on evidence admissibility.

HISTORICAL NOTE
Source:
Federal Rules of Evidence, Rule 607.
Fed.Rules Civ.Proc., Rule 43(b), 28 U.S.C.A.
Code 1939, § 21-922.
Rule Civ.Proc., former Rule 43(g).
17A Pt. 1 A. R. S. Rules of Evid., Rule 607, AZ ST REV Rule 607
Current with amendments received through 11/1/17

Rule 608. A Witness's Character for Truthfulness or Untruthfulness

Currentness

(a) Reputation or Opinion Evidence. A witness's credibility may be attacked or supported by testimony about the witness's reputation for having a character for truthfulness or untruthfulness, or by testimony in the form of an opinion about that character. But evidence of truthful character is admissible only after the witness's character for truthfulness has been attacked.

(b) Specific Instances of Conduct. Except for a criminal conviction under Rule 609, extrinsic evidence is not admissible to prove specific instances of a witness's conduct in order to attack or support the witness's character for truthfulness. But the court may, on cross-examination, allow them to be inquired into if they are probative of the character for truthfulness or untruthfulness of:

(1) the witness; or

(2) another witness whose character the witness being cross-examined has testified about.

By testifying on another matter, a witness does not waive any privilege against self-incrimination for testimony that relates only to the witness's character for truthfulness.

Credits

Amended Oct. 19, 1988, effective Nov. 1, 1988; Sept. 8, 2011, effective Jan. 1, 2012.

Editors' Notes

COMMENT TO 2012 AMENDMENT

This rule has been amended to conform to Federal Rule of Evidence 608, including changing two references to "credibility" to "character for truthfulness" in subsection (b). Additionally, the language of Rule 608 has been amended to conform to the federal restyling of the Evidence Rules to make them more easily understood and to make style and terminology consistent throughout the rules. These changes are intended to be stylistic only. There is no intent in the restyling to change any result in any ruling on evidence admissibility.

COMMENT TO ORIGINAL 1977 RULE

State v. Superior Court, 113 Ariz. 22, 545 P.2d 946 (1976) is consistent with and interpretative of Rule 608(b).

COMMENT

State v. Superior Court, 113 Ariz. 22, 545 P.2d 946 (1976) is consistent with and interpretative of Rule 608(b).

HISTORICAL NOTE

Source:

Fed.Rules Civ.Proc., Rule 43(b), 28 U.S.C.A.

Code 1939, § 21-922.

Rule Civ.Proc., former Rule 43(g).

Federal Rules of Evidence, Rule 608.

17A Pt. 1 A. R. S. Rules of Evid., Rule 608, AZ ST REV Rule 608

Current with amendments received through 11/1/17

Rule 609. Impeachment by Evidence of a Criminal Conviction

<u>Currentness</u>

(a) In General. The following rules apply to attacking a witness's character for truthfulness by evidence of a criminal conviction:

(1) for a crime that, in the convicting jurisdiction, was punishable by death or by imprisonment for more than one year, the evidence:

(A) must be admitted, subject to Rule 403, in a civil case or in a criminal case in which the witness is not a defendant; and

(B) must be admitted in a criminal case in which the witness is a defendant, if the probative value of the evidence outweighs its prejudicial effect to that defendant; and

(2) for any crime regardless of the punishment, the evidence must be admitted if the court can readily determine that establishing the elements of the crime required proving--or the witness's admitting--a dishonest act or false statement.

(b) Limit on Using the Evidence After 10 Years. This subsection (b) applies if more than 10 years have passed since the witness's conviction or release from confinement for it, whichever is later. Evidence of the conviction is admissible only if:

(1) its probative value, supported by specific facts and circumstances, substantially outweighs its prejudicial effect; and

(2) the proponent gives an adverse party reasonable written notice of the intent to use it so that the party has a fair opportunity to contest its use.

(c) Effect of a Pardon, Annulment, or Certificate of Rehabilitation. Evidence of a conviction is not admissible if:

(1) the conviction has been the subject of a pardon, annulment, certificate of rehabilitation, or other equivalent procedure based on a finding that the person has been rehabilitated, and the person has not been convicted of a later crime punishable by death or by imprisonment for more than one year; or

(2) the conviction has been the subject of a pardon, annulment, or other equivalent procedure based on a finding of innocence.

(d) Juvenile Adjudications. Evidence of a juvenile adjudication is admissible under this rule only if:

(1) it is offered in a criminal case;

(2) the adjudication was of a witness other than the defendant;

(3) an adult's conviction for that offense would be admissible to attack the adult's credibility; and

(4) admitting the evidence is necessary to fairly determine guilt or innocence.

(e) Pendency of an Appeal. A conviction that satisfies this rule is admissible even if an appeal is pending. Evidence of the pendency is also admissible.

Credits

Amended Oct. 19, 1988, effective Nov. 1, 1988; Sept. 8, 2011, effective Jan. 1, 2012.

Editors' Notes

COMMENT TO 2012 AMENDMENT

This rule has been amended to conform to Federal Rule of Evidence 609, including changing "credibility" to "character for truthfulness" in subsection (a), and adding language to the last clause of subdivision (a)(2) to clarify that this evidence must be admitted "if the court can readily determine that establishing the elements of the crime required proving--or the witness's admitting--a dishonest act or false statement." Additionally, the language of Rule 609 has been amended to conform to the federal restyling of the Evidence Rules to make them more easily understood and to make style and terminology consistent throughout the rules. These changes are intended to be stylistic only. There is no intent in the restyling to change any result in any ruling on evidence admissibility.

COMMENT TO ORIGINAL 1977 RULE

Subsection (d) is contrary to the provisions of A.R.S. § 8-207, but in criminal cases due process may require that the fact of a juvenile adjudication be admitted to show the existence of possible bias and prejudice. Davis v. Alaska, 415 U.S. 308, 94 S.Ct. 1105, 39 L.Ed.2d 347 (1974). The fact of a juvenile delinquency adjudication may not be used to impeach the general credibility of a witness. The admission of such evidence may be necessary to meet due process standards.

HISTORICAL NOTE

Source:

Federal Rules of Evidence, Rule 609.

Fed.Rules Civ.Proc., Rule 43(b), 28 U.S.C.A.

Code 1939, § 21-922.

Rule Civ.Proc., former Rule 43(g).

17A Pt. 1 A. R. S. Rules of Evid., Rule 609, AZ ST REV Rule 609

Current with amendments received through 11/1/17

Rule 610. Religious Beliefs or Opinions

Currentness

Evidence of a witness's religious beliefs or opinions is not admissible to attack or support the witness's credibility.

Credits

Amended Oct. 19, 1988, effective Nov. 1, 1988; Sept. 8, 2011, effective Jan. 1, 2012.

Editors' Notes

COMMENT TO 2012 AMENDMENT

The language of Rule 610 has been amended to conform to the federal restyling of the Evidence Rules to make them more easily understood and to make style and terminology consistent throughout the rules. These changes are intended to be stylistic only. There is no intent to change any result in any ruling on evidence admissibility.

HISTORICAL NOTE

Source:

Federal Rules of Evidence, Rule 610.

17A Pt. 1 A. R. S. Rules of Evid., Rule 610, AZ ST REV Rule 610

Current with amendments received through 11/1/17

Rule 611. Mode and Order of Examining Witnesses and Presenting Evidence

Currentness

(a) Control by the Court; Purposes. The court should exercise reasonable control over the mode and order of examining witnesses and presenting evidence so as to:

(1) make those procedures effective for determining the truth;

(2) avoid wasting time; and

(3) protect witnesses from harassment or undue embarrassment.

(b) Scope of cross-examination. A witness may be cross-examined on any relevant matter.

(c) Leading Questions. Leading questions should not be used on direct examination except as necessary to develop the witness's testimony. Ordinarily, the court should allow leading questions:

(1) on cross-examination; and

(2) when a party calls a hostile witness, an adverse party, or a witness identified with an adverse party.

Credits

Amended Oct. 19, 1988, effective Nov. 1, 1988; Oct. 24, 1995, effective Dec. 1, 1995; Sept. 8, 2011, effective Jan. 1, 2012.

Editors' Notes

COMMENT TO 2012 AMENDMENT

This rule has been amended to conform to Federal Rule of Evidence 611, except for subsection (b), which has not been changed.

Additionally, the language of subsections (a) and (c) has been amended to conform to the federal restyling of the Evidence Rules to make them more easily understood and to make style and terminology consistent throughout the rules. These changes are intended to be stylistic only. There is no intent in the restyling to change any result in any ruling on evidence admissibility.

The 2012 amendment of Rule 611(a) is not intended to diminish a trial court's ability to impose reasonable time limits on trial proceedings, which is otherwise provided for by rules of procedure. Similarly, the 2012 amendment of Rule 611(c) is not intended to change existing practice under which a witness called on direct examination and interrogated by leading questions may be interrogated by leading questions on behalf of the adverse party as well.

COMMENT TO RULE 611(A), 1995 AMENDMENT

Following are suggested procedures for effective document control:

(1) The trial judge should become involved as soon as possible, and no later than the pretrial conference, in controlling the number of documents to be used at trial.

(2) For purposes of trial, only one number should be applied to a document whenever referred to.

(3) Copies of key trial exhibits should be provided to the jurors for temporary viewing or for keeping in juror notebooks.

(4) Exhibits with text should and, on order of the court, shall be highlighted to direct jurors' attention to important language. Where important to an understanding of the document, that language should be explained during the course of trial.

(5) At the close of evidence in a trial involving numerous exhibits, the trial judge shall ensure that a simple and clear retrieval system, e.g., an index, is provided to the jurors to assist them in finding exhibits during deliberations.

COMMENT TO ORIGINAL 1977 RULE

The last sentence of (c) changes the Arizona Supreme Court's holding in J. & B. Motors, Inc. v. Margolis, 75 Ariz. 392, 257 P.2d 588 (1953).

HISTORICAL NOTE

Source:

Federal Rules of Evidence, Rule 611.

Fed.Rules Civ.Proc., Rule 43(b), 28 U.S.C.A.

Code 1939, § 21-922.

Rules Civ.Proc., former Rule 43(g).
17A Pt. 1 A. R. S. Rules of Evid., Rule 611, AZ ST REV Rule 611
Current with amendments received through 11/1/17

Rule 612. Writing Used to Refresh a Witness's Memory

Currentness
(a) Scope. This rule gives an adverse party certain options when a witness uses a writing to refresh memory:
(1) while testifying; or
(2) before testifying, if the court decides that justice requires the party to have those options.
(b) Adverse Party's Options; Deleting Unrelated Matter. An adverse party is entitled to have the writing produced at the hearing, to inspect it, to cross-examine the witness about it, and to introduce in evidence any portion that relates to the witness's testimony. If the producing party claims that the writing includes unrelated matter, the court must examine the writing in camera, delete any unrelated portion, and order that the rest be delivered to the adverse party. Any portion deleted over objection must be preserved for the record.
(c) Failure to Produce or Deliver the Writing. If a writing is not produced or is not delivered as ordered, the court may issue any appropriate order. But if the prosecution does not comply in a criminal case, the court must strike the witness's testimony or--if justice so requires--declare a mistrial.
Credits
Amended Oct. 19, 1988, effective Nov. 1, 1988; Sept. 8, 2011, effective Jan. 1, 2012.
Editors' Notes
COMMENT TO 2012 AMENDMENT
The language of Rule 612 has been amended to conform to the federal restyling of the Evidence Rules to make them more easily understood and to make style and terminology consistent throughout the rules. These changes are intended to be stylistic only. There is no intent to change any result in any ruling on evidence admissibility.
COMMENT TO ORIGINAL 1977 RULE
Subparagraphs (1) and (2) of Federal Rule 612 have been reversed in order to clarify the intent of the rule which is to invoke the court's discretion concerning matters used before testifying and to have production as a matter of right of materials used while testifying. The word "action" in the second sentence of the rule replaces "testimony" in the Federal Rule to accord with the broader scope of cross-examination used in Arizona.
HISTORICAL NOTE
Source:
Federal Rules of Evidence, Rule 612, (modified).
17A Pt. 1 A. R. S. Rules of Evid., Rule 612, AZ ST REV Rule 612
Current with amendments received through 11/1/17

Rule 613. Witness's Prior Statements of Witnesses

Currentness

(a) Showing or Disclosing the Statement During Examination. When examining a witness about the witness's prior statement, a party need not show it or disclose its contents to the witness. But the party must, on request, show it or disclose its contents to an adverse party's attorney.

(b) Extrinsic Evidence of a Prior Inconsistent Statement. Extrinsic evidence of a witness's prior inconsistent statement is admissible only if the witness is given an opportunity to explain or deny the statement and an adverse party is given an opportunity to examine the witness about it, or if justice so requires. This subdivision (b) does not apply to an opposing party's statement under Rule 801(d)(2).

Credits

Amended Oct. 19, 1988, effective Nov. 1, 1988; Sept. 8, 2011, effective Jan. 1, 2012.

Editors' Notes

COMMENT TO 2012 AMENDMENT

The language of Rule 613 has been amended to conform to the federal restyling of the Evidence Rules to make them more easily understood and to make style and terminology consistent throughout the rules. These changes are intended to be stylistic only. There is no intent to change any result in any ruling on evidence admissibility.

HISTORICAL NOTE

Source:

Federal Rules of Evidence, Rule 613.

Fed.Rules Civ.Proc., Rule 43(b), 28 U.S.C.A.

Code 1939, § 21-922.

Rule Civ.Proc., former Rule 43(g).

17A Pt. 1 A. R. S. Rules of Evid., Rule 613, AZ ST REV Rule 613

Current with amendments received through 11/1/17

Rule 614. Court's Calling or Examining a Witnesses

Currentness

(a) Calling. The court may call a witness on its own or at a party's request. Each party is entitled to cross-examine the witness.

(b) Examining. The court may examine a witness regardless of who calls the witness.

(c) Objections. A party may object to the court's calling or examining a witness either at that time or at the next opportunity when the jury is not present.

Credits

Amended Sept. 8, 2011, effective Jan. 1, 2012.

Editors' Notes

COMMENT TO 2012 AMENDMENT

The language of Rule 614 has been amended to conform to the federal restyling of the Evidence Rules to make them more easily understood and to make style and terminology consistent throughout the rules. These changes are intended to be stylistic only. There is no intent to change any result in any ruling on evidence admissibility.

HISTORICAL NOTE

Source:

Federal Rules of Evidence, Rule 614.

17A Pt. 1 A. R. S. Rules of Evid., Rule 614, AZ ST REV Rule 614

Current with amendments received through 11/1/17

Rule 615. Excluding Witnesses

Currentness

At a party's request, the court must order witnesses excluded so that they cannot hear other witnesses' testimony. Or the court may do so on its own. But this rule does not authorize excluding:

(a) a party who is a natural person;

(b) an officer or employee of a party that is not a natural person, after being designated as the party's representative by its attorney;

(c) a person whose presence a party shows to be essential to presenting the party's claim or defense;

(d) a person authorized by statute to be present; or

(e) a victim of crime, as defined by applicable law, who wishes to be present during proceedings against the defendant.

Credits

Amended Oct. 19, 1988, effective Nov. 1, 1988; Nov. 12, 1991, effective Dec. 31, 1991; Sept. 8, 2011, effective Jan. 1, 2012.

Editors' Notes

COMMENT TO 2012 AMENDMENT

This rule has been amended to conform to Federal Rule of Evidence 615, including the addition of subsection (d).

Subsection (e) (formerly subsection (d)), which is a uniquely Arizona provision, has been retained but amended to reflect that "a victim of crime" means a crime victim "as defined by applicable law," which includes any applicable rule, statute, or constitutional provision. The rule previously provided that "a victim of crime" would be "as defined by Rule 39(a), Rules of Criminal Procedure."

Additionally, the language of Rule 615 has been amended to conform to the federal restyling of the Evidence Rules to make them more easily understood and to make style and terminology consistent throughout the rules. These changes are intended to be stylistic only. There is no intent in the restyling to change any result in any ruling on evidence admissibility.

COMMENT TO 1991 AMENDMENT

The 1991 amendment to Rule 615 was necessary in order to conform the rule to the victim's right to be present at criminal proceedings, recognized in Ariz. Const. Art. II, § 2.1(A)(3).

HISTORICAL NOTE

Source:

Article VII.☐ Opinions and Expert Testimony

Introductory Note to Original 1977 Rules: Problems of Opinion Testimony

Currentness

The rules in this article are designed to avoid unnecessary restrictions concerning the admissibility of opinion evidence; however, as this note makes clear, an adverse attorney may, by timely objection, invoke the court's power to require that before admission of an opinion there be a showing of the traditional evidentiary prerequisites. Generally, it is not intended that evidence which would have been inadmissible under pre-existing law should now become admissible.

A major objective of these rules is to eliminate or sharply reduce the use of hypothetical questions. With these rules, hypothetical questions should seldom be needed and the court will be expected to exercise its discretion to curtail the use of hypothetical questions as inappropriate and premature jury summations. Ordinarily, a qualified expert witness can be asked whether he has an opinion on a particular subject and then what that opinion is. If an objection is made and the court determines that the witness should disclose the underlying facts or data before giving the opinion, the witness should identify the facts or data necessary to the opinion.

In jury trials, if there is an objection and if facts or data upon which opinions are to be based have not been admitted in evidence at the time the opinion is offered, the court may admit the opinion subject to later admission of the underlying facts or data; however, the court will be expected to exercise its discretion so as to prevent the admission of such opinions if there is any serious question concerning the admissibility, under Rule 703 or otherwise, of the underlying facts or data.

17A Pt. 1 A. R. S. Rules of Evid., Art. 7 Introduction, AZ ST REV Art. 7 Introduction
Current with amendments received through 11/1/17

Rule 701. Opinion Testimony by Lay Witnesses

Currentness

If a witness is not testifying as an expert, testimony in the form of an opinion is limited to one that is:

(a) rationally based on the witness's perception;

(b) helpful to clearly understanding the witness's testimony or to determining a fact in issue; and

(c) not based on scientific, technical, or other specialized knowledge within the scope of Rule 702.

Credits

Amended Oct. 19, 1988, effective Nov. 1, 1988; Sept. 8, 2011, effective Jan. 1, 2012.

Editors' Notes

COMMENT TO 2012 AMENDMENT

The 2012 amendment of Rule 701 adopts Federal Rule of Evidence 701, as restyled.

HISTORICAL NOTE

Source:

Federal Rules of Evidence, Rule 701.

17A Pt. 1 A. R. S. Rules of Evid., Rule 701, AZ ST REV Rule 701

Current with amendments received through 11/1/17

Rule 702. Testimony by Expert Witnesses

<u>Currentness</u>

A witness who is qualified as an expert by knowledge, skill, experience, training, or education may testify in the form of an opinion or otherwise if:

(a) the expert's scientific, technical, or other specialized knowledge will help the trier of fact to understand the evidence or to determine a fact in issue;

(b) the testimony is based on sufficient facts or data;

(c) the testimony is the product of reliable principles and methods; and

(d) the expert has reliably applied the principles and methods to the facts of the case.

Credits

Amended Sept. 8, 2011, effective Jan. 1, 2012.

Editors' Notes

COMMENT TO 2012 AMENDMENT

The 2012 amendment of Rule 702 adopts Federal Rule of Evidence 702, as restyled. The amendment recognizes that trial courts should serve as gatekeepers in assuring that proposed expert testimony is reliable and thus helpful to the jury's determination of facts at issue. The amendment is not intended to supplant traditional jury determinations of credibility and the weight to be afforded otherwise admissible testimony, nor is the amendment intended to permit a challenge to the testimony of every expert, preclude the testimony of experience-based experts, or prohibit testimony based on competing methodologies within a field of expertise. The trial court's gatekeeping function is not intended to replace the adversary system. Cross-examination, presentation of contrary evidence, and careful instruction on the burden of proof are the traditional and appropriate means of attacking shaky but admissible evidence.

A trial court's ruling finding an expert's testimony reliable does not necessarily mean that contradictory expert testimony is not reliable. The amendment is broad enough to permit testimony that is the product of competing principles or methods in the same field of expertise. Where there is contradictory, but reliable, expert testimony, it is the province of the jury to determine the weight and credibility of the testimony.

This comment has been derived, in part, from the Committee Notes on Rules--2000 Amendment to Federal Rule of Evidence 702.

HISTORICAL NOTE

Source:

Rule 703. Bases of an Expert's Opinion Testimony

<u>Currentness</u>

An expert may base an opinion on facts or data in the case that the expert has been made aware of or personally observed. If experts in the particular field would reasonably rely on those kinds of facts or data in forming an opinion on the subject, they need not be admissible for the opinion to be admitted. But if the facts or data would otherwise be inadmissible, the proponent of the opinion may disclose them to the jury only if their probative value in helping the jury evaluate the opinion substantially outweighs their prejudicial effect.

Credits

Amended Oct. 19, 1988, effective Nov. 1, 1988; Sept. 3, 2009, effective Jan. 1, 2010; Sept. 8, 2011, effective Jan. 1, 2012.

Editors' Notes

COMMENT TO 2012 AMENDMENT

The language of Rule 703 has been amended to conform to the federal restyling of the Evidence Rules to make them more easily understood and to make style and terminology consistent throughout the rules. These changes are intended to be stylistic only. There is no intent to change any result in any ruling on evidence admissibility.

All references to an "inference" have been deleted on the grounds that the deletion made the rule flow better and easier to read, and because any "inference" is covered by the broader term "opinion." Courts have not made substantive decisions on the basis of any distinction between an opinion and an inference. No change in current practice is intended.

COMMENT TO ORIGINAL 1977 RULE

This rule, along with others in this article, is designed to expedite the reception of expert testimony. Caution is urged in its use. Particular attention is called to the Advisory Committee's Note to the Federal Rules of Evidence which accompanies Federal Rule 703. In addition, it should be emphasized that the standard "if of a type reasonably relied upon by experts in the particular field" is applicable to both sentences of the rule. The question of whether the facts or data are of a type reasonably relied upon by experts is in all instances a question of law to be resolved by the court prior to the admission of the evidence. If the facts or data meet this standard and form the basis of admissible opinion evidence they become admissible under this rule for the limited purpose of disclosing the basis for the opinion unless they should be excluded pursuant to an applicable constitutional provision, statute, rule or decision.

Evidence which is inadmissible except as it may qualify as being "reasonably relied upon by experts in the particular field" has traditionally included such things as certain medical reports and comparable sales in condemnation actions.

HISTORICAL NOTE

Source:

Federal Rules of Evidence, Rule 703.
17A Pt. 1 A. R. S. Rules of Evid., Rule 703, AZ ST REV Rule 703
Current with amendments received through 11/1/17

Rule 703. Bases of an Expert's Opinion Testimony

Currentness

An expert may base an opinion on facts or data in the case that the expert has been made aware of or personally observed. If experts in the particular field would reasonably rely on those kinds of facts or data in forming an opinion on the subject, they need not be admissible for the opinion to be admitted. But if the facts or data would otherwise be inadmissible, the proponent of the opinion may disclose them to the jury only if their probative value in helping the jury evaluate the opinion substantially outweighs their prejudicial effect.

Credits

Amended Oct. 19, 1988, effective Nov. 1, 1988; Sept. 3, 2009, effective Jan. 1, 2010; Sept. 8, 2011, effective Jan. 1, 2012.

Editors' Notes

COMMENT TO 2012 AMENDMENT

The language of Rule 703 has been amended to conform to the federal restyling of the Evidence Rules to make them more easily understood and to make style and terminology consistent throughout the rules. These changes are intended to be stylistic only. There is no intent to change any result in any ruling on evidence admissibility.

All references to an "inference" have been deleted on the grounds that the deletion made the rule flow better and easier to read, and because any "inference" is covered by the broader term "opinion." Courts have not made substantive decisions on the basis of any distinction between an opinion and an inference. No change in current practice is intended.

COMMENT TO ORIGINAL 1977 RULE

This rule, along with others in this article, is designed to expedite the reception of expert testimony. Caution is urged in its use. Particular attention is called to the Advisory Committee's Note to the Federal Rules of Evidence which accompanies Federal Rule 703. In addition, it should be emphasized that the standard "if of a type reasonably relied upon by experts in the particular field" is applicable to both sentences of the rule. The question of whether the facts or data are of a type reasonably relied upon by experts is in all instances a question of law to be resolved by the court prior to the admission of the evidence. If the facts or data meet this standard and form the basis of admissible opinion evidence they become admissible under this rule for the limited purpose of disclosing the basis for the opinion unless they should be excluded pursuant to an applicable constitutional provision, statute, rule or decision.

Evidence which is inadmissible except as it may qualify as being "reasonably relied upon by experts in the particular field" has traditionally included such things as certain medical reports and comparable sales in condemnation actions.

HISTORICAL NOTE

Source:

Federal Rules of Evidence, Rule 703.
17A Pt. 1 A. R. S. Rules of Evid., Rule 703, AZ ST REV Rule 703
Current with amendments received through 11/1/17

Rule 704. Opinion on an Ultimate Issue

Currentness

(a) In General--Not Automatically Objectionable. An opinion is not objectionable just because it embraces an ultimate issue.

(b) Exception. In a criminal case, an expert witness must not state an opinion about whether the defendant did or did not have a mental state or condition that constitutes an element of the crime charged or of a defense. Those matters are for the trier of fact alone.

Credits
Amended Sept. 8, 2011, effective Jan. 1, 2012.

Editors' Notes

COMMENT TO 2012 AMENDMENT
Subsection (b) has been added to conform to Federal Rule of Evidence 704, which was amended in 1984 to add comparable language. The new language in the Arizona rule is considered to be consistent with current Arizona law.

Additionally, the language of Rule 704 has been amended to conform to the federal restyling of the Evidence Rules to make them more easily understood and to make style and terminology consistent throughout the rules. These changes are intended to be stylistic only. There is no intent in the restyling to change any result in any ruling on evidence admissibility.

The Court deleted the reference to an "inference" on the grounds that the deletion made the rule flow better and easier to read, and because any "inference" is covered by the broader term "opinion." Courts have not made substantive decisions on the basis of any distinction between an opinion and an inference. No change in current practice is intended.

COMMENT TO ORIGINAL 1977 RULE
Some opinions on ultimate issues will be rejected as failing to meet the requirement that they assist the trier of fact to understand the evidence or to determine a fact in issue. Witnesses are not permitted as experts on how juries should decide cases.

HISTORICAL NOTE
Source:
Federal Rules of Evidence, Rule 704.
17A Pt. 1 A. R. S. Rules of Evid., Rule 704, AZ ST REV Rule 704
Current with amendments received through 11/1/17

Rule 705. Disclosing the Facts or Data Underlying an Expert's Opinion

Unless the court orders otherwise, an expert may state an opinion--and give the reasons for it--without first testifying to the underlying facts or data. But the expert may be required to disclose those facts or data on cross-examination.

Credits

Amended Oct. 19, 1988, effective Nov. 1, 1988; Sept. 3, 2009, effective Jan. 1, 2010; Sept. 8, 2011, effective Jan. 1, 2012.

Editors' Notes

COMMENT TO 2012 AMENDMENT

The language of Rule 705 has been amended to conform to the federal restyling of the Evidence Rules to make them more easily understood and to make style and terminology consistent throughout the rules. These changes are intended to be stylistic only. There is no intent to change any result in any ruling on evidence admissibility. The reference to an "inference" has been deleted on the grounds that the deletion made the rule flow better and easier to read, and because any "inference" is covered by the broader term "opinion." Courts have not made substantive decisions on the basis of any distinction between an opinion and an inference. No change in current practice is intended.

HISTORICAL NOTE

Source:

Federal Rules of Evidence, Rule 705.

17A Pt. 1 A. R. S. Rules of Evid., Rule 705, AZ ST REV Rule 705

Current with amendments received through 11/1/17

Rule 706. Court Appointed Expert Witnesses

(a) Appointment Process. On a party's motion or on its own, the court may order the parties to show cause why expert witnesses should not be appointed and may ask the parties to submit nominations. The court may appoint any expert that the parties agree on and any of its own choosing. But the court may only appoint someone who consents to act.

(b) Expert's Role. The court must inform the expert of the expert's duties. The court may do so in writing and have a copy filed with the clerk or may do so orally at a conference in which the parties have an opportunity to participate. The expert:

(1) must advise the parties of any findings the expert makes;

(2) may be deposed by any party;

(3) may be called to testify by the court or any party; and

(4) may be cross-examined by any party, including the party that called the expert.

(c) Compensation. The expert is entitled to a reasonable compensation, as set by the court. Except as otherwise provided by law, appointment of an expert by the court is subject to the availability of funds or the agreement of the parties concerning compensation.

(d) Disclosing the Appointment to the Jury. The court may authorize disclosure to the jury that the court appointed the expert.

(e) Parties' Choice of Their Own Experts. This rule does not limit a party in calling its own experts.

Credits

Amended Oct. 19, 1988, effective Nov. 1, 1988; Sept. 8, 2011, effective Jan. 1, 2012.

Editors' Notes

COMMENT TO 2012 AMENDMENT

The language of subsection (c) of Rule 706 has been amended to provide, consistent with Federal Rule of Evidence 706, that an expert is entitled to a reasonable compensation, as set by the court.

Additionally, the language of subsections (a), (b), (d), and (e) of the rule has been amended to conform to the federal restyling of the Evidence Rules to make them more easily understood and to make style and terminology consistent throughout the rules. These changes are intended to be stylistic only. There is no intent in the restyling to change any result in any ruling on evidence admissibility.

COMMENT TO ORIGINAL 1977 RULE

Federal Rules of Evidence, Rule 706(b) is appropriate in Federal Courts where the funds to compensate experts are made available by statute. Such funds are not generally available in Arizona except in capital offenses, A.R.S. § 13-673; sanity hearings, A.R.S. § 13-1674; medical liability review panels, A.R.S. § 12-567(B)(4) and (M); and mental health proceedings, A.R.S. § 36-545.04. Therefore, Arizona Rules of Evidence, Rule 706(a) was prefaced by the availability of these funds or the compensation of the experts to be agreed upon, and Federal Rules of Evidence, Rule 706(b) was not adopted, and paragraphs numbered (c) and (d) were renumbered paragraphs (b) and (c) respectively.

HISTORICAL NOTE

Source:

Federal Rules of Evidence, Rule 706, (modified).

17A Pt. 1 A. R. S. Rules of Evid., Rule 706, AZ ST REV Rule 706

Current with amendments received through 11/1/17

Article VIII.☐ Hearsay

Rule 801. Definitions That Apply to This Article; Exclusions from Hearsay

Currentness

(a) Statement. "Statement" means a person's oral assertion, written assertion, or nonverbal conduct, if the person intended it as an assertion.

(b) Declarant. "Declarant" means the person who made the statement.

(c) Hearsay. "Hearsay" means a statement that:

(1) the declarant does not make while testifying at the current trial or hearing; and

(2) a party offers in evidence to prove the truth of the matter asserted in the statement.

(d) Statements That Are Not Hearsay. A statement that meets the following conditions is not hearsay:

(1) *A Declarant-Witness's Prior Statement.* The declarant testifies and is subject to cross-examination about a prior statement, and the statement:

(A) is inconsistent with the declarant's testimony;

(B) is consistent with the declarant's testimony and is offered:

(i) to rebut an express or implied charge that the declarant recently fabricated it or acted from a recent improper influence or motive in so testifying; or

(ii) to rehabilitate the declarant's credibility as a witness when attacked on another ground; or

(C) identifies a person as someone the declarant perceived earlier.

(2) *An Opposing Party's Statement.* The statement is offered against an opposing party and:

(A) was made by the party in an individual or representative capacity;

(B) is one the party manifested that it adopted or believed to be true;

(C) was made by a person whom the party authorized to make a statement on the subject;

(D) was made by the party's agent or employee on a matter within the scope of that relationship and while it existed; or

(E) was made by the party's coconspirator during and in furtherance of the conspiracy.

The statement must be considered but does not by itself establish the declarant's authority under (C); the existence or scope of the relationship under (D); or the existence of the conspiracy or participation in it under (E).

Credits

Amended Oct. 19, 1988, effective Nov. 1, 1988; Sept. 8, 2011, effective Jan. 1, 2012; Sept. 2, 2014, effective Jan. 1, 2015.

Editors' Notes

COMMENT TO 2015 AMENDMENT TO RULE 801(D)(1)(B)

Rule 801(d)(1)(B), as originally adopted, provided for substantive use of certain prior consistent statements of a witness subject to cross-examination. As the federal Advisory Committee on Evidence Rules noted, "[t]he prior statement is consistent with the testimony given on the stand, and, if the opposite party wishes to open the door for its admission in evidence, no sound reason is apparent why it should not be received generally."

Though the original Rule 801(d)(1)(B) provided for substantive use of certain prior consistent statements, the scope of that rule was limited. The rule covered only those consistent statements that were offered to rebut charges of recent fabrication or improper motive or influence. The rule did not, for example, provide for substantive admissibility of consistent statements that are probative to explain what otherwise appears to be an inconsistency in the witness's testimony. Nor did it cover consistent statements that would be probative to rebut a charge of faulty memory.

The amendment retains the requirement set forth in *Tome v. United States,* 513 U.S. 150 (1995): that under Rule 801(d)(1)(B), a consistent statement offered to rebut a charge of recent fabrication or improper influence or motive must have been made before the alleged fabrication or improper inference or motive arose. The intent of the amendment is to extend substantive effect to consistent statements that rebut other attacks on a witness -- such as the charges of inconsistency or faulty memory. The amendment does not change the traditional and well-accepted limits on bringing prior consistent statements before the factfinder for credibility purposes. It does not allow impermissible bolstering of a witness. As before, prior consistent statements under the amendment may be brought before the factfinder only if they properly rehabilitate a witness whose credibility has been attacked. As before, to be admissible for rehabilitation, a prior consistent statement must satisfy the strictures of Rule 403. As before, the trial court has ample discretion to exclude prior consistent statements that are cumulative accounts of an event.

COMMENT TO 2012 AMENDMENT

The last sentence of Rule 801(d)(2) has been added to conform to Federal Rule of Evidence 801(d)(2). The amendment does not, however, include the requirement in Federal Rule of Evidence 801(d)(1)(A) that a prior inconsistent statement be "given under oath" to be considered as non-hearsay.

Otherwise, the language of Rule 801 has been amended to conform to the federal restyling of the Evidence Rules to make them more easily understood and to make style and terminology consistent throughout the rules. These changes are intended to be stylistic only. There is no intent in the restyling to change any result in any ruling on evidence admissibility.

Statements falling under the hearsay exclusion provided by Rule 801(d)(2) are no longer referred to as "admissions" in the title to the subdivision. The term "admissions" is confusing because not all statements covered by the exclusion are admissions in the colloquial sense--a statement can be within the exclusion even if it "admitted" nothing and was not against the party's interest when made. The term "admissions" also raises confusion in comparison with the Rule 804(b)(3) exception for declarations against interest. No change in application of the exclusion is intended.

COMMENT TO ORIGINAL 1977 RULE

Evidence which is admissible under the hearsay rules may be inadmissible under some other rule or principle. A notable example is the confrontation clause of the Constitution as applied to criminal cases. The definition of "hearsay" is a utilitarian one. The exceptions to the hearsay rule are based upon considerations of reliability, need, and experience. Like all other rules which favor the admission of evidence, the exceptions to the hearsay rule are counterbalanced by Rules 102 and 403.

Rule 801(d). This subsection of the rule has been modified and is consistent with the United States Supreme Court's version of the Rule and State v. Skinner, 110 Ariz. 135, 515 P.2d 880 (1973).

HISTORICAL NOTE

Source:

Federal Rules of Evidence, Rule 801, (modified).

17A Pt. 1 A. R. S. Rules of Evid., Rule 801, AZ ST REV Rule 801

Current with amendments received through 11/1/17

Rule 802. The Rule Against Hearsay

Hearsay is not admissible unless any of the following provides otherwise:

• an applicable constitutional provision or statute;

• these rules; or

• other rules prescribed by the Supreme Court.

Credits

Amended Sept. 8, 2011, effective Jan. 1, 2012.

Editors' Notes

COMMENT ON 2012 AMENDMENT

The language of Rule 802 has been amended to conform to the federal restyling of the Evidence Rules to make them more easily understood and to make style and terminology consistent throughout the rules. These changes are intended to be stylistic only. There is no intent to change any result in any ruling on evidence admissibility.

HISTORICAL NOTE

Source:

Federal Rules of Evidence, Rule 802, (modified).

17A Pt. 1 A. R. S. Rules of Evid., Rule 802, AZ ST REV Rule 802

Current with amendments received through 11/1/17

Rule 803. Exceptions to the Rule Against Hearsay--Regardless of Whether the Declarant Is Available as a Witness

The following are not excluded by the rule against hearsay, regardless of whether the declarant is available as a witness:

(1) Present Sense Impression. A statement describing or explaining an event or condition, made while or immediately after the declarant perceived it.

(2) Excited Utterance. A statement relating to a startling event or condition, made while the declarant was under the stress of excitement that it caused.

(3) Then-Existing Mental, Emotional, or Physical Condition. A statement of the declarant's then-existing state of mind (such as motive, intent, or plan) or emotional, sensory, or physical condition (such as mental feeling, pain, or bodily health), but not including a statement of memory or belief to prove the fact remembered or believed unless it relates to the validity or terms of the declarant's will.

(4) Statement Made for Medical Diagnosis or Treatment. A statement that:

(A) is made for--and is reasonably pertinent to--medical diagnosis or treatment; and

(B) describes medical history; past or present symptoms or sensations; their inception; or their general cause.

(5) Recorded Recollection. A record that:

(A) is on a matter the witness once knew about but now cannot recall well enough to testify fully and accurately;

(B) was made or adopted by the witness when the matter was fresh in the witness's memory; and

(C) accurately reflects the witness's knowledge.

If admitted, the record may be read into evidence but may be received as an exhibit only if offered by an adverse party.

(6) Records of a Regularly Conducted Activity. A record of an act, event, condition, opinion, or diagnosis if:

(A) the record was made at or near the time by -- or from information transmitted by -- someone with knowledge;

(B) the record was kept in the course of a regularly conducted activity of a business, organization, occupation, or calling, whether or not for profit;

(C) making the record was a regular practice of that activity;

(D) all these conditions are shown by the testimony of the custodian or another qualified witness, or by a certification that complies with Rule 902(11) or (12) or with a statute permitting certification; and

(E) the opponent does not show that the source of information or the method or circumstances of preparation indicate a lack of trustworthiness.

(7) Absence of a Record of a Regularly Conducted Activity. Evidence that a matter is not included in a record described in paragraph (6) if:

(A) the evidence is admitted to prove that the matter did not occur or exist;

(B) a record was regularly kept for a matter of that kind; and

(C) the opponent does not show that the possible source of the information or other circumstances indicate a lack of trustworthiness.

(8) Public Records. A record or statement of a public office if:

(A) it sets out:

(i) the office's activities;

(ii) a matter observed while under a legal duty to report, but not including, in a criminal case, a matter observed by law-enforcement personnel; or

(iii) in a civil case or against the government in a criminal case, factual findings from a legally authorized investigation; and

(B) the opponent does not show that the source of information or other circumstances indicate a lack of trustworthiness.

(9) Public Records of Vital Statistics. A record of a birth, death, or marriage, if reported to a public office in accordance with a legal duty.

(10) Absence of a Public Record. Testimony--or a certification under Rule 902--that a diligent search failed to disclose a public record or statement if

(A) the testimony or certification is admitted to prove that

(i) the record or statement does not exist; or

(ii) a matter did not occur or exist, if a public office regularly kept a record or statement for a matter of that kind; and

(B) in a criminal case, a prosecutor who intends to offer a certification provides written notice of that intent at least 20 days before trial, and the defendant does not object in writing within 10 days of receiving the notice--unless the court sets a different time for the notice or the objection.

(11) Records of Religious Organizations Concerning Personal or Family History. A statement of birth, legitimacy, ancestry, marriage, divorce, death, relationship by blood or marriage, or similar facts of personal or family history, contained in a regularly kept record of a religious organization.

(12) Certificates of Marriage, Baptism, and Similar Ceremonies. A statement of fact contained in a certificate:

(A) made by a person who is authorized by a religious organization or by law to perform the act certified;

(B) attesting that the person performed a marriage or similar ceremony or administered a sacrament; and

(C) purporting to have been issued at the time of the act or within a reasonable time after it.

(13) Family Records. A statement of fact about personal or family history contained in a family record, such as a Bible, genealogy, chart, engraving on a ring, inscription on a portrait, or engraving on an urn or burial marker.

(14) Records of Documents That Affect an Interest in Property. The record of a document that purports to establish or affect an interest in property if:

(A) the record is admitted to prove the content of the original recorded document, along with its signing and its delivery by each person who purports to have signed it;

(B) the record is kept in a public office; and

(C) a statute authorizes recording documents of that kind in that office.

(15) Statements in Documents That Affect an Interest in Property. A statement contained in a document that purports to establish or affect an interest in property if the matter stated was relevant to the document's purpose -- unless later dealings with the property are inconsistent with the truth of the statement or the purport of the document.

(16) Statements in Ancient Documents. A statement in a document that was prepared before January 1, 1998, and whose authenticity is established.

(17) Market Reports and Similar Commercial Publications. Market quotations, lists, directories, or other compilations that are generally relied on by the public or by persons in particular occupations.

(18) Statements in Learned Treatises, Periodicals, or Pamphlets. A statement contained in a treatise, periodical, or pamphlet if:

(A) the statement is called to the attention of an expert witness on cross-examination or relied on by the expert on direct examination; and

(B) the publication is established as a reliable authority by the expert's admission or testimony, by another expert's testimony, or by judicial notice.

If admitted, the statement may be read into evidence but not received as an exhibit.

(19) Reputation Concerning Personal or Family History. A reputation among a person's family by blood, adoption, or marriage--or among a person's associates or in the community--concerning the person's birth, adoption, legitimacy, ancestry, marriage, divorce, death, relationship by blood, adoption, or marriage, or similar facts of personal or family history.

(20) Reputation Concerning Boundaries or General History. A reputation in a community--arising before the controversy--concerning boundaries of land in the community or customs that affect the land, or concerning general historical events important to that community, state, or nation.

(21) Reputation Concerning Character. A reputation among a person's associates or in the community concerning the person's character.

(22) Judgment of a Previous Conviction. Evidence of a final judgment of conviction if:

(A) the judgment was entered after a trial or guilty plea, but not a nolo contendere plea;

(B) the conviction was for a crime punishable by death or by imprisonment for more than a year;

(C) the evidence is admitted to prove any fact essential to the judgment; and

(D) when offered by the prosecutor in a criminal case for a purpose other than impeachment, the judgment was against the defendant.

The pendency of an appeal may be shown but does not affect admissibility.

(23) Judgments Involving Personal, Family, or General History or a Boundary. A judgment that is admitted to prove a matter of personal, family, or general history, or boundaries, if the matter:

(A) was essential to the judgment; and

(B) could be proved by evidence of reputation.

(24) [Other exceptions.] [Transferred to Rule 807.]

(25) Former testimony (non-criminal action or proceeding). Except in a criminal action or proceeding, testimony given as a witness at another hearing of the same or different proceeding, or in a deposition taken in compliance with law in the course of the same or another proceeding, if the party against whom the testimony is now offered, or a predecessor in interest, had an opportunity and similar motive to develop the testimony by direct, cross, or redirect examination.

Credits

Amended Oct. 19, 1988, effective Nov. 1, 1988; Oct. 3, 1994, effective Dec. 1, 1994; Oct. 16, 2003, effective Dec. 1, 2003; Sept. 8, 2011, effective Jan. 1, 2012; Aug. 28, 2013, effective Jan. 1, 2014; Sept. 2, 2014, effective Jan. 1, 2015; Aug. 31, 2017, effective Jan. 1, 2018.

Editors' Notes

COMMENT TO 2018 AMENDMENT TO RULE 803(16)

The ancient documents exception to the rule against hearsay has been limited to statements in documents prepared before January 1, 1998. The Court has determined that the ancient documents exception should be limited due to the risk that it will be used as a vehicle to admit vast amounts of unreliable electronically stored information (ESI). Given the exponential development and growth of electronic information since 1998, the hearsay exception for ancient documents has now become a possible open door for large amounts of unreliable ESI, as no showing of reliability needs to be made to qualify under the exception.

The Court is aware that in certain cases--such as cases involving latent diseases and environmental damage--parties must rely on hardcopy documents from the past. The ancient documents exception remains available for such cases for documents prepared before 1998. Going forward, it is anticipated that any need to admit old hardcopy documents produced after January 1, 1998 will decrease, because reliable ESI is likely to be available and can be offered under a reliability-based hearsay exception. Rule 803(6) may be used for many of these ESI documents, especially given its flexible standards on which witnesses might be qualified to provide an adequate foundation. And Rule 807 can be used to admit old documents upon a showing of reliability--which will often (though not always) be found by circumstances such as that the document was prepared with no litigation motive in mind, close in time to the relevant events. The limitation of the ancient documents exception is not intended to raise an inference that 20 year-old documents are, as a class, unreliable, or that they should somehow not qualify for admissibility under Rule 807. Finally, many old documents can be admitted for the non-hearsay purpose of proving notice, or as party-opponent statements. Under the amendment, a document is "prepared" when the statement proffered was recorded in that document. For example, if a hardcopy document is prepared in 1995, and a party seeks to admit a scanned copy of that document, the date of preparation is 1995 even though the scan was made long after that--the subsequent scan does not alter the document. The relevant point is the date on which the information is recorded, not when the information is prepared for trial. However, if the content of the document is *itself* altered after the cut-off date, then the hearsay exception will not apply to statements that were added in the alteration.

COMMENT TO 2015 AMENDMENT TO RULE 803(6)

The rule has been amended to clarify that if the proponent has established the stated requirements of the exception -- regular business with regularly kept record, source with personal knowledge, record made timely, and foundation testimony or certification -- then the burden is on the opponent to show that the source of information or the method or circumstances of preparation indicate a lack of trustworthiness. It is appropriate to impose this burden on opponent, as the basic admissibility requirements are sufficient to establish a presumption that the record is reliable.

The opponent, in meeting its burden, is not necessarily required to introduce affirmative evidence of untrustworthiness. For example, the opponent might argue that a record was prepared in anticipation of litigation and is favorable to the preparing party without needing to introduce evidence on the point. A determination of untrustworthiness necessarily depends on the circumstances.

COMMENT TO 2015 AMENDMENT TO RULE 803(7)

The rule has been amended to clarify that if the proponent has established the stated requirements of the exception -- set forth in Rule 803(6) -- then the burden is on the opponent to show that the possible source of the information or other circumstances indicate a lack of trustworthiness. The amendment maintains consistency with the amendment to the trustworthiness clause of Rule 803(6).

COMMENT TO 2015 AMENDMENT TO RULE 803(8)

The rule has been amended to clarify that if the proponent has established that the record meets the stated requirements of the exception -- prepared by a public office and setting out information as specified in the rule -- then the burden is on the opponent to show that the source of information or other circumstances indicate a lack of trustworthiness. Public records have justifiably carried a presumption of reliability. The amendment maintains consistency with the amendment to the trustworthiness clause of Rule 803(6).

COMMENT TO 2014 AMENDMENT

Rule 803(10) has been amended to incorporate, with minor variations, a "'notice-and-demand" procedure that was approved in *Melendez-Diaz v. Massachusetts,* 129 S. Ct. 2527 (2009). This amendment is not intended to alter any otherwise applicable disclosure requirements.

COMMENT TO 2012 AMENDMENT

To conform to Federal Rule of Evidence 803(6)(A), as restyled, the language "first hand knowledge" in Rule 803(6)(b) has been changed to "knowledge" in amended Rule 803(6)(A). The new language is not intended to change the requirement that the record be made by--or from information transmitted by--someone with personal or first hand knowledge.

To conform to Federal Rules of Evidence 803(24) and 807, Rule 803(24) has been deleted and transferred to Rule 807.

Rule 803(25) has not been amended to conform to the federal rules.

Otherwise, the language of Rule 803 has been amended to conform to the federal restyling of the Evidence Rules to make them more easily understood and to make style and terminology consistent throughout the rules. These changes are intended to be stylistic only. There is no intent in the restyling to change any result in any ruling on evidence admissibility.

COMMENT TO 1994 AMENDMENT

For provisions governing former testimony in criminal actions or proceedings, *see* Rule 804(b)(1) and Rule 19.3(c), Rules of Criminal Procedure.

HISTORICAL NOTE

Source:

Federal Rules of Evidence, Rule 803, (modified).

Civ.Code 1901, § 2546.

Civ.Code 1913, §§ 1734, 1736, 1743, 1756, 1757.

Rev.Code 1928, §§ 4452, 4456, 4463.

Fed.Rules Civ.Proc., Rule 44(c), 28 U.S.C.A.

Code 1939, §§ 21-928, 23-303, 23-307.

Laws 1951, Ch. 62, § 1.

Code 1939, Supp.1952, § 23-314.

Rules Civ.Proc., former Rules 44(e), 44(f), 44(i), 44(q), 44(s).

17A Pt. 1 A. R. S. Rules of Evid., Rule 803, AZ ST REV Rule 803

Current with amendments received through 11/1/17

Rule 804. Exceptions to the Rule Against Hearsay--When the Declarant Is Unavailable as a Witness

Currentness

(a) Criteria for Being Unavailable. A declarant is considered to be unavailable as a witness if the declarant:

(1) is exempted from testifying about the subject matter of the declarant's statement because the court rules that a privilege applies;

(2) refuses to testify about the subject matter despite a court order to do so;

(3) testifies to not remembering the subject matter;

(4) cannot be present or testify at the trial or hearing because of death or a then-existing infirmity, physical illness, or mental illness; or

(5) is absent from the trial or hearing and the statement's proponent has not been able, by process or other reasonable means, to procure:

(A) the declarant's attendance, in the case of a hearsay exception under Rule 804(b)(1) or (6); or

(B) the declarant's attendance or testimony, in the case of a hearsay exception under Rule 804(b)(2), (3), or (4).

But this subsection (a) does not apply if the statement's proponent procured or wrongfully caused the declarant's unavailability as a witness in order to prevent the declarant from attending or testifying.

(b) The Exceptions. The following are not excluded by the rule against hearsay if the declarant is unavailable as a witness:

(1) *Former Testimony in a Criminal Case.* Testimony that:

(A) was made under oath by a party or witness during a previous judicial proceeding or a deposition under Arizona Rule of Criminal Procedure 15.3 shall be admissible in evidence if:

(i) The party against whom the former testimony is offered was a party to the action or proceeding during which a statement was given and had the right and opportunity to cross-examine the declarant with an interest and motive similar to that which the party now has (no person who was unrepresented by counsel at the proceeding during which a statement was made shall be deemed to have had the right and opportunity to cross-examine the declarant, unless such representation was waived) and

(ii) The declarant is unavailable as a witness, or is present and subject to cross-examination.

(B) The admissibility of former testimony under this subsection is subject to the same limitations and objections as though the declarant were testifying at the hearing, except that the former testimony offered under this subsection is not subject to:

(i) Objections to the form of the question which were not made at the time the prior testimony was given.

(ii) Objections based on competency or privilege which did not exist at the time the former testimony was given.

(2) *Statement Under the Belief of Imminent Death.* In a prosecution for homicide or in a civil case, a statement that the declarant, while believing the declarant's death to be imminent, made about its cause or circumstances.

(3) *Statement Against Interest.* A statement that:

(A) a reasonable person in the declarant's position would have made only if the person believed it to be true because, when made, it was so contrary to the declarant's proprietary or pecuniary interest or had so great a tendency to invalidate the declarant's claim against someone else or to expose the declarant to civil or criminal liability; and

(B) is supported by corroborating circumstances that clearly indicate its trustworthiness, if it is offered in a criminal case as one that tends to expose the declarant to criminal liability.

(4) *Statement of Personal or Family History.* A statement about:

(A) the declarant's own birth, adoption, legitimacy, ancestry, marriage, divorce, relationship by blood, adoption, or marriage, or similar facts of personal or family history, even though the declarant had no way of acquiring personal knowledge about that fact; or

(B) another person concerning any of these facts, as well as death, if the declarant was related to the person by blood, adoption, or marriage or was so intimately associated with the person's family that the declarant's information is likely to be accurate.

(5) [Formerly (7) *Other exceptions.*] [Transferred to Rule 807.]

(6) *Statement Offered Against a Party That Wrongfully Caused the Declarant's Unavailability.* A statement offered against a party that wrongfully caused--or acquiesced in wrongfully causing--the declarant's unavailability as a witness, and did so intending that result.

Credits
Amended Oct. 19, 1988, effective Nov. 1, 1988; Oct. 3, 1994, effective Dec. 1, 1994; Sept. 3, 2009, effective Jan. 1, 2010; Sept. 8, 2011, effective Jan. 1, 2012.

Editors' Notes
COMMENT TO 2012 AMENDMENT
Rule 804(b)(3) has been amended to conform to Federal Rule of Evidence 804(b)(3), as amended effective December 1, 2010.

To conform to Federal Rules of Evidence 804(b)(5) and 807, Rule 804(b)(7) has been deleted and transferred to Rule 807.

Rule 804(b)(1) has been amended to incorporate the language of Arizona Rule of Criminal Procedure 19.3(c), but has not been amended to conform to the federal rules. Otherwise, the language of Rule 804 has been amended to conform to the federal restyling of the Evidence Rules to make them more easily understood and to make style and terminology consistent throughout the rules. These changes are intended to be stylistic only. There is no intent in the restyling to change any result in any ruling on evidence admissibility.

COMMENT TO 1994 AMENDMENT
For provisions governing former testimony in non-criminal actions or proceedings, *see* Rule 803(25).

HISTORICAL NOTE
Source:
Federal Rules of Evidence, Rule 804.
17A Pt. 1 A. R. S. Rules of Evid., Rule 804, AZ ST REV Rule 804
Current with amendments received through 11/1/17

Rule 805. Hearsay Within Hearsay

Currentness

Hearsay within hearsay is not excluded by the rule against hearsay if each part of the combined statements conforms with an exception to the rule.

Credits
Amended Sept. 8, 2011, effective Jan. 1, 2012.

Editors' Notes
COMMENT TO 2012 AMENDMENT
The language of Rule 805 has been amended to conform to the federal restyling of the Evidence Rules to make them more easily understood and to make style and terminology consistent throughout the rules. These changes are intended to be stylistic only. There is no intent to change any result in any ruling on evidence admissibility.

HISTORICAL NOTE
Source:
Federal Rules of Evidence, Rule 805.

END OF DOCUMENT

Rule 805. Hearsay Within Hearsay

Currentness

Hearsay within hearsay is not excluded by the rule against hearsay if each part of the combined statements conforms with an exception to the rule.

Credits

Amended Sept. 8, 2011, effective Jan. 1, 2012.

Editors' Notes

COMMENT TO 2012 AMENDMENT

The language of Rule 805 has been amended to conform to the federal restyling of the Evidence Rules to make them more easily understood and to make style and terminology consistent throughout the rules. These changes are intended to be stylistic only. There is no intent to change any result in any ruling on evidence admissibility.

HISTORICAL NOTE

Source:

Federal Rules of Evidence, Rule 805.

17A Pt. 1 A. R. S. Rules of Evid., Rule 805, AZ ST REV Rule 805
Current with amendments received through 11/1/17

Rule 806. Attacking and Supporting the Declarant's Credibility

Currentness

When a hearsay statement--or a statement described in Rule 801(d)(2)(C), (D), or (E)--has been admitted in evidence, the declarant's credibility may be attacked, and then supported, by any evidence that would be admissible for those purposes if the declarant had testified as a witness. The court may admit evidence of the declarant's inconsistent statement or conduct, regardless of when it occurred or whether the declarant had an opportunity to explain or deny it. If the party against whom the statement was admitted calls the declarant as a witness, the party may examine the declarant on the statement as if on cross-examination.

Credits

Amended Oct. 19, 1988, effective Nov. 1, 1988; Sept. 8, 2011, effective Jan. 1, 2012.

Editors' Notes

COMMENT TO 2012 AMENDMENT

The language of Rule 806 has been amended to conform to the federal restyling of the Evidence Rules to make them more easily understood and to make style and terminology consistent throughout the rules. These changes are intended to be stylistic only. There is no intent to change any result in any ruling on evidence admissibility.

HISTORICAL NOTE
Source:
Federal Rules of Evidence, Rule 806.
17A Pt. 1 A. R. S. Rules of Evid., Rule 806, AZ ST REV Rule 806
Current with amendments received through 11/1/17

Rule 807. Residual Exception

Currentness

(a) In General. Under the following circumstances, a hearsay statement is not excluded by the rule against hearsay even if the statement is not specifically covered by a hearsay exception in Rule 803 or 804:

(1) the statement has equivalent circumstantial guarantees of trustworthiness;

(2) it is offered as evidence of a material fact;

(3) it is more probative on the point for which it is offered than any other evidence that the proponent can obtain through reasonable efforts; and

(4) admitting it will best serve the purposes of these rules and the interests of justice.

(b) Notice. The statement is admissible only if, before the trial or hearing, the proponent gives an adverse party reasonable notice of the intent to offer the statement and its particulars, including the declarant's name and address, so that the party has a fair opportunity to meet it.

Credits
Added Sept. 8, 2011, effective Jan. 1, 2012.

Editors' Notes
COMMENT TO 2012 AMENDMENT
Rule 807 has been adopted to conform to Federal Rule of Evidence 807, as restyled.

17A Pt. 1 A. R. S. Rules of Evid., Rule 807, AZ ST REV Rule 807
Current with amendments received through 11/1/17

Article IX.☐ Authentication and Identification

Rule 901. Authenticating and Identifying Evidence

Currentness

(a) In General. To satisfy the requirement of authenticating or identifying an item of evidence, the proponent must produce evidence sufficient to support a finding that the item is what the proponent claims it is.

(b) Examples. The following are examples only--not a complete list--of evidence that satisfies the requirement:

(1) *Testimony of a Witness with Knowledge.* Testimony that an item is what it is claimed to be.

(2) *Nonexpert Opinion About Handwriting.* A nonexpert's opinion that handwriting is genuine, based on a familiarity with it that was not acquired for the current litigation.

(3) *Comparison by an Expert Witness or the Trier of Fact.* A comparison with an authenticated specimen by an expert witness or the trier of fact.

(4) *Distinctive Characteristics and the Like.* The appearance, contents, substance, internal patterns, or other distinctive characteristics of the item, taken together with all the circumstances.

(5) *Opinion About a Voice.* An opinion identifying a person's voice--whether heard firsthand or through mechanical or electronic transmission or recording--based on hearing the voice at any time under circumstances that connect it with the alleged speaker.

(6) *Evidence About a Telephone Conversation.* For a telephone conversation, evidence that a call was made to the number assigned at the time to:

(A) a particular person, if circumstances, including self-identification, show that the person answering was the one called; or

(B) a particular business, if the call was made to a business and the call related to business reasonably transacted over the telephone.

(7) *Evidence About Public Records.* Evidence that:

(A) a document was recorded or filed in a public office as authorized by law; or

(B) a purported public record or statement is from the office where items of this kind are kept.

(8) *Evidence About Ancient Documents or Data Compilations.* For a document or data compilation, evidence that it:

(A) is in a condition that creates no suspicion about its authenticity;

(B) was in a place where, if authentic, it would likely be; and

(C) is at least 20 years old when offered.

(9) *Evidence About a Process or System.* Evidence describing a process or system and showing that it produces an accurate result.

(10) *Methods Provided by a Statute or Rule.* Any method of authentication or identification allowed by a statute or a rule prescribed by the Supreme Court.

Credits

Amended Sept. 8, 2011, effective Jan. 1, 2012.

Editors' Notes

COMMENT TO 2012 AMENDMENT

The language of Rule 901 has been amended to conform to the federal restyling of the Evidence Rules to make them more easily understood and to make style and terminology consistent throughout the rules. These changes are intended to be stylistic only. There is no intent to change any result in any ruling on evidence admissibility.

COMMENT TO ORIGINAL 1977 RULE

This rule is declaratory of general evidence law and deals only with identification or authentication and not with grounds for admissibility.

HISTORICAL NOTE

Source:

Federal Rules of Evidence, Rule 901.

Civ.Code 1901, §§ 2544, 2547.

Civ.Code 1913, §§ 1735, 1741, 1744, 1748, 1756, 1757.

Rev.Code 1928, §§ 4453, 4455, 4457, 4460, 4463.
Fed.Rules Civ.Proc., Rule 44(c), 28 U.S.C.A.
Code 1939, §§ 21-928, 23-304, 23-306, 23-308, 23-311.
Laws 1951, Ch. 62, § 1.
Code 1939, Supp.1952, § 23-314.
Rules Civ.Proc., former Rules 44(i), 44(j), 44(*l*), 44(m), 44(n), 44(r).
17A Pt. 1 A. R. S. Rules of Evid., Rule 901, AZ ST REV Rule 901
Current with amendments received through 11/1/17

Rule 902. Evidence That Is Self-Authenticating

Currentness

The following items of evidence are self-authenticating; they require no extrinsic evidence of authenticity in order to be admitted:

(1) Domestic Public Documents That Are Sealed and Signed. A document that bears:

(A) a seal purporting to be that of the United States; any state, district, commonwealth, territory, or insular possession of the United States; the former Panama Canal Zone; the Trust Territory of the Pacific Islands; a political subdivision of any of these entities; or a department, agency, or officer of any entity named above; and

(B) a signature purporting to be an execution or attestation.

(2) Domestic Public Documents That Are Not Sealed but Are Signed and Certified. A document that bears no seal if:

(A) it bears the signature of an officer or employee of an entity named in Rule 902(1)(A); and

(B) another public officer who has a seal and official duties within that same entity certifies under seal--or its equivalent--that the signer has the official capacity and that the signature is genuine.

(3) Foreign Public Documents. A document that purports to be signed or attested by a person who is authorized by a foreign country's law to do so. The document must be accompanied by a final certification that certifies the genuineness of the signature and official position of the signer or attester--or of any foreign official whose certificate of genuineness relates to the signature or attestation or is in a chain of certificates of genuineness relating to the signature or attestation. The certification may be made by a secretary of a United States embassy or legation; by a consul general, vice consul, or consular agent of the United States; or by a diplomatic or consular official of the foreign country assigned or accredited to the United States. If all parties have been given a reasonable opportunity to investigate the document's authenticity and accuracy, the court may, for good cause, either:

(A) order that it be treated as presumptively authentic without final certification; or

(B) allow it to be evidenced by an attested summary with or without final certification.

(4) Certified Copies of Public Records. A copy of an official record--or a copy of a document that was recorded or filed in a public office as authorized by law--if the copy is certified as correct by:

(A) the custodian or another person authorized to make the certification; or

(B) a certificate that complies with Rule 902(1), (2), or (3), a statute, or a rule prescribed by the Supreme Court.

(5) Official Publications. A book, pamphlet, or other publication purporting to be issued by a public authority.

(6) Newspapers and Periodicals. Printed material purporting to be a newspaper or periodical.

(7) Trade Inscriptions and the Like. An inscription, sign, tag, or label purporting to have been affixed in the course of business and indicating origin, ownership, or control.

(8) Acknowledged Documents. A document accompanied by a certificate of acknowledgment that is lawfully executed by a notary public or another officer who is authorized to take acknowledgments.

(9) Commercial Paper and Related Documents. Commercial paper, a signature on it, and related documents, to the extent allowed by general commercial law.

(10) Presumptions Under a Statute. A signature, document, or anything else that a statute declares to be presumptively or prima facie genuine or authentic.

(11) Certified Domestic Records of a Regularly Conducted Activity. The original or a copy of a domestic record that meets the requirements of Rule 803(6)(A)-(C), as shown by a certification of the custodian or another qualified person that complies with a statute or a rule prescribed by the Supreme Court. Before the trial or hearing, the proponent must give an adverse party reasonable written notice of the intent to offer the record--and must make the record and certification available for inspection--so that the party has a fair opportunity to challenge them.

(12) Certified Foreign Records of a Regularly Conducted Activity. In a civil case, the original or a copy of a foreign record that meets the requirements of Rule 902(11), modified as follows: the certification, rather than complying with a statute or Supreme Court rule, must be signed in a manner that, if falsely made, would subject the maker to a criminal penalty in the country where the certification is signed. The proponent must also meet the notice requirements of Rule 902(11).

(13) Certified Records Generated by an Electronic Process or System. A record generated by an electronic process or system that produces an accurate result, as shown by a certification of a qualified person that complies with the certification requirements of Rule 902(11) or (12). The proponent must also meet the notice requirements of Rule 902(11).

(14) Certified Data Copied from an Electronic Device, Storage Medium, or File. Data copied from an electronic device, storage medium, or file, if authenticated by a process of digital identification, as shown by a certification of a qualified person that complies with the certification requirements of Rule 902(11) or (12). The proponent also must meet the notice requirements of Rule 902(11).

Credits

Amended Oct. 19, 1988, effective Nov. 1, 1988; Oct. 16, 2003, effective Dec. 1, 2003; Jan. 26, 2004, effective June 1, 2004; Sept. 8, 2011, effective Jan. 1, 2012; Aug. 31, 2017, effective Jan. 1, 2018.

Editors' Notes

COMMENT TO 2018 AMENDMENT ADDING SUBDIVISION (13)

The amendment sets forth a procedure by which parties can authenticate certain electronic evidence other than through the testimony of a foundation witness. As with the provisions on business records in Rules 902(11) and (12), the Court has determined that the expense and inconvenience of producing a witness to authenticate an item of electronic evidence is often unnecessary. It is often the case that a party goes to the expense of producing an authentication witness and then the adversary either stipulates authenticity before the witness is called or fails to challenge the authentication testimony once it is presented. The amendment provides a procedure under which the parties can determine in advance of trial whether a real challenge to authenticity will be made, and can then plan accordingly.

A proponent establishing authenticity under this Rule must present a certification containing information that would be sufficient to establish authenticity were that information provided by a witness at trial. If the certification provides information that would be insufficient to authenticate the record if the certifying person testified, then authenticity is not established under this Rule. The Rule specifically allows the authenticity foundation that satisfies Rule 901(b)(9) to be established by a certification rather than the testimony of a live witness.

The reference to the "certification requirements of Rule 902(11) or (12)" is only to the procedural requirements for a valid certification. There is no intent to require, or permit, a certification under this rule to prove the requirements of Rule 803(6). Rule 902(13) is solely limited to authentication and any attempt to satisfy a hearsay exception must be made independently.

In order to provide the adverse party with an opportunity to properly analyze the issue of authenticity, the "record" provided by the proponent of the ESI evidence must include the metadata for the material in question if reasonably necessary to assess the material's authenticity. In addition, a challenge to the authenticity of electronic evidence may require technical information about the system or process at issue, including possibly retaining a forensic technical expert; such factors will affect whether the opponent has a fair opportunity to challenge the evidence given the notice provided.

COMMENT TO 2018 AMENDMENT ADDING SUBDIVISION (14)

The amendment sets forth a procedure by which parties can authenticate data copied from an electronic device, storage medium, or an electronic file, other than through the testimony of a foundation witness. As with the provisions on business records in Rules 902(11) and (12), the Court has determined that the expense and inconvenience of producing an authenticating witness for this evidence is often unnecessary. It is often the case that a party goes to the expense of producing an authentication witness, and then the adversary either stipulates authenticity before the witness is called or fails to challenge the authentication testimony once it is presented. The amendment provides a procedure in which the parties can determine in advance of trial whether a real challenge to authenticity will be made, and can then plan accordingly.

Today, data copied from electronic devices, storage media, and electronic files are ordinarily authenticated by "hash value." A hash value is a number that is often represented as a sequence of characters and is produced by an algorithm based upon the digital contents of a drive, medium, or file. If the hash values for the original and copy are different, then the copy is not identical to the original. If the hash values for the original and copy are the same, it is highly improbable that the original and copy are not identical. Thus, identical hash values for the original and copy reliably attest to the fact that they are exact duplicates. This amendment allows self-authentication by a certification of a qualified person that the person checked the hash value of the proffered item and that it was identical to the original. The rule is flexible enough to allow certifications through processes other than comparison of hash value, including by other reliable means of identification provided by future technology.

In order to provide the adverse party with an opportunity to properly analyze the issue of authenticity, the "record" provided by the proponent of the ESI evidence must include the metadata for the material in question if reasonably necessary to assess the material's authenticity. In addition, a challenge to the authenticity of electronic evidence may require technical information about the system or process at issue, including possibly retaining a forensic technical expert; such factors will affect whether the opponent has a fair opportunity to challenge the evidence given the notice provided.

COMMENT TO 2012 AMENDMENT

The language of Rule 902 has been amended to conform to the federal restyling of the Evidence Rules to make them more easily understood and to make style and terminology consistent throughout the rules. These changes are intended to be stylistic only. There is no intent to change any result in any ruling on evidence admissibility.

COMMENT TO ORIGINAL 1977 RULE

The language "general commercial law" in (9) is carried forward from the Federal Rule. In Arizona, the reference is to the Uniform Commercial Code as adopted in this State.

HISTORICAL NOTE

Source:

Federal Rules of Evidence, Rule 902.

Civ.Code 1901, § 2548.

Civ.Code 1913, §§ 1734, 1736, 1745, 1748.

Laws 1921, Ch. 2, § 1.

Rev.Code 1928, §§ 4450, 4452, 4458, 4460.

Fed.Rules Civ.Proc., Rule 44(a), 28 U.S.C.A.

Code 1939, §§ 21-926, 23-301, 23-303, 23-309, 23-311.

Rules Civ.Proc., former Rules 44(b), 44(d), 44(e), 44(g), 44(j).

17A Pt. 1 A. R. S. Rules of Evid., Rule 902, AZ ST REV Rule 902

Current with amendments received through 11/1/17

Rule 903. Subscribing Witness's Testimony

Currentness

A subscribing witness's testimony is necessary to authenticate a writing only if required by the law of the jurisdiction that governs its validity.

Credits

Amended Sept. 8, 2011, effective Jan. 1, 2012.

Editors' Notes

COMMENT TO 2012 AMENDMENT

The language of Rule 903 has been amended to conform to the federal restyling of the Evidence Rules to make them more easily understood and to make style and terminology consistent throughout the rules. These changes are intended to be stylistic only. There is no intent to change any result in any ruling on evidence admissibility.

HISTORICAL NOTE
Source:
Federal Rules of Evidence, Rule 903.
Laws 1921, Ch. 2, § 1.
Rev.Code 1928, § 4450.
Code 1939, § 23-301.
Rules Civ.Proc., former Rule 44(d).
17A Pt. 1 A. R. S. Rules of Evid., Rule 903, AZ ST REV Rule 903
Current with amendments received through 11/1/17

Article X.☐ Contents of Writings, Recordings, and Photographs

Rule 1001. Definitions That Apply to This Article

Currentness

In this article:

(a) A "writing" consists of letters, words, numbers, or their equivalent set down in any form.

(b) A "recording" consists of letters, words, numbers, or their equivalent recorded in any manner.

(c) A "photograph" means a photographic image or its equivalent stored in any form.

(d) An "original" of a writing or recording means the writing or recording itself or any counterpart intended to have the same effect by the person who executed or issued it. For electronically stored information, "original" means any printout--or other output readable by sight--if it accurately reflects the information. An "original" of a photograph includes the negative or a print from it.

(e) A "duplicate" means a counterpart produced by a mechanical, photographic, chemical, electronic, or other equivalent process or technique that accurately reproduces the original.

Credits
Amended Sept. 8, 2011, effective Jan. 1, 2012.

Editors' Notes
COMMENT TO 2012 AMENDMENT
The language of Rule 1001 has been amended to conform to the federal restyling of the Evidence Rules to make them more easily understood and to make style and terminology consistent throughout the rules. These changes are intended to be stylistic only. There is no intent to change any result in any ruling on evidence admissibility.

HISTORICAL NOTE
Source:
Federal Rules of Evidence, Rule 1001.
Civ.Code 1913, §§ 1756, 1757.
Rev.Code 1928, § 4463.
Laws 1951, Ch. 62, § 1.
Code 1939, Supp.1952, § 23-314.

Rules Civ.Proc., former Rule 44(s).
17A Pt. 1 A. R. S. Rules of Evid., Rule 1001, AZ ST REV Rule 1001
Current with amendments received through 11/1/17

Rule 1002. Requirement of the Original

Currentness
An original writing, recording, or photograph is required in order to prove its content unless these rules or an applicable statute provides otherwise.

Credits
Amended Sept. 8, 2011, effective Jan. 1, 2012.

Editors' Notes
COMMENT TO 2012 AMENDMENT
The language of Rule 1002 has been amended to conform to the federal restyling of the Evidence Rules to make them more easily understood and to make style and terminology consistent throughout the rules. These changes are intended to be stylistic only. There is no intent to change any result in any ruling on evidence admissibility.
HISTORICAL NOTE
Source:
Federal Rules of Evidence, Rule 1002, (modified).
Civ.Code 1913, §§ 1756, 1757.
Rev.Code 1928, § 4463.
Laws 1951, Ch. 62, § 1.
Code 1939, Supp.1952, § 23-314.
Rules Civ.Proc., former Rule 44(s).
17A Pt. 1 A. R. S. Rules of Evid., Rule 1002, AZ ST REV Rule 1002
Current with amendments received through 11/1/17

Rule 1003. Admissibility of Duplicates

Currentness
A duplicate is admissible to the same extent as the original unless a genuine question is raised about the original's authenticity or the circumstances make it unfair to admit the duplicate.

Credits
Amended Sept. 8, 2011, effective Jan. 1, 2012.

Editors' Notes
COMMENT TO 2012 AMENDMENT
The language of Rule 1003 has been amended to conform to the federal restyling of the Evidence Rules to make them more easily understood and to make style and terminology consistent throughout the rules. These changes are intended to be stylistic only. There is no intent to change any result in any ruling on evidence admissibility.
HISTORICAL NOTE

Rule 1004. Admissibility of Other Evidence of Contents

Currentness

An original is not required and other evidence of the content of a writing, recording, or photograph is admissible if:

(a) all the originals are lost or destroyed, and not by the proponent acting in bad faith;

(b) an original cannot be obtained by any available judicial process;

(c) the party against whom the original would be offered had control of the original; was at that time put on notice, by pleadings or otherwise, that the original would be a subject of proof at the trial or hearing; and fails to produce it at the trial or hearing; or

(d) the writing, recording, or photograph is not closely related to a controlling issue.

Credits

Amended Oct. 19, 1988, effective Nov. 1, 1988; Sept. 8, 2011, effective Jan. 1, 2012.

Editors' Notes

COMMENT TO 2012 AMENDMENT

The language of Rule 1004 has been amended to conform to the federal restyling of the Evidence Rules to make them more easily understood and to make style and terminology consistent throughout the rules. These changes are intended to be stylistic only. There is no intent to change any result in any ruling on evidence admissibility.

HISTORICAL NOTE

Source:

Federal Rules of Evidence, Rule 1004.

Fed.Rules Civ.Proc., Rules 44(b), 44(c), 28 U.S.C.A.

Code 1939, §§ 21-927, 21-928.

Rules Civ.Proc., former Rules 44(h), 44(i).

17A Pt. 1 A. R. S. Rules of Evid., Rule 1004, AZ ST REV Rule 1004

Current with amendments received through 11/1/17

Rule 1005. Copies of Public Records to Prove Content

Currentness

The proponent may use a copy to prove the content of an official record--or of a document that was recorded or filed in a public office as authorized by law--if these conditions are met: the record or document is otherwise admissible; and the copy is certified as correct in accordance with Rule 902(4) or is testified to be correct by a witness who has compared it with the original. If no such copy can be obtained by reasonable diligence, then the proponent may use other evidence to prove the content.

Credits

Amended Sept. 8, 2011, effective Jan. 1, 2012.

Editors' Notes

COMMENT TO 2012 AMENDMENT

The language of Rule 1005 has been amended to conform to the federal restyling of the Evidence Rules to make them more easily understood and to make style and terminology consistent throughout the rules. These changes are intended to be stylistic only. There is no intent to change any result in any ruling on evidence admissibility.

HISTORICAL NOTE

Source:

Federal Rules of Evidence, Rule 1005.

Civ.Code 1901, §§ 2546 to 2548.

Civ.Code 1913, §§ 1735, 1743 to 1745.

Rev.Code 1928, §§ 4453, 4456 to 4458.

Fed.Rules Civ.Proc., Rule 44(a), 28 U.S.C.A.

Code 1939, §§ 21-926, 23-304, 23-307 to 23-309.

Rules Civ.Proc., former Rules 44(b), 44(f), 44(g), 44(l), 44(n).

17A Pt. 1 A. R. S. Rules of Evid., Rule 1005, AZ ST REV Rule 1005

Current with amendments received through 11/1/17

Rule 1006. Summaries to Prove Content

Currentness

The proponent may use a summary, chart, or calculation to prove the content of voluminous writings, recordings, or photographs that cannot be conveniently examined in court. The proponent must make the originals or duplicates available for examination or copying, or both, by other parties at a reasonable time and place. And the court may order the proponent to produce them in court.

Credits

Amended Sept. 8, 2011, effective Jan. 1, 2012.

Editors' Notes

COMMENT TO 2012 AMENDMENT

The language of Rule 1006 has been amended to conform to the federal restyling of the Evidence Rules to make them more easily understood and to make style and terminology consistent throughout the rules. These changes are intended to be stylistic only. There is no intent to change any result in any ruling on evidence admissibility.

COMMENT TO ORIGINAL 1977 RULE

This rule is not intended to change foundation requirements for summaries. The person creating a summary will ordinarily be required to lay the foundation and be available for cross-examination.

HISTORICAL NOTE

Source:

Federal Rules of Evidence, Rule 1006.

17A Pt. 1 A. R. S. Rules of Evid., Rule 1006, AZ ST REV Rule 1006

Current with amendments received through 11/1/17

Rule 1007. Testimony or Statement of a Party to Prove Content

The proponent may prove the content of a writing, recording, or photograph by the testimony, deposition, or written statement of the party against whom the evidence is offered. The proponent need not account for the original.

Credits

Amended Oct. 19, 1988, effective Nov. 1, 1988; Sept. 8, 2011, effective Jan. 1, 2012.

Editors' Notes

COMMENT TO 2012 AMENDMENT

The language of Rule 1007 has been amended to conform to the federal restyling of the Evidence Rules to make them more easily understood and to make style and terminology consistent throughout the rules. These changes are intended to be stylistic only. There is no intent to change any result in any ruling on evidence admissibility.

HISTORICAL NOTE

Source:

Federal Rules of Evidence, Rule 1007.

17A Pt. 1 A. R. S. Rules of Evid., Rule 1007, AZ ST REV Rule 1007

Current with amendments received through 11/1/17

Rule 1008. Functions of the Court and Jury

Ordinarily, the court determines whether the proponent has fulfilled the factual conditions for admitting other evidence of the content of a writing, recording, or photograph under Rule 1004 or 1005. But in a jury trial, the jury determines--in accordance with Rule 104(b)--any issue about whether:

(a) an asserted writing, recording, or photograph ever existed;

(b) another one produced at the trial or hearing is the original; or

(c) other evidence of content accurately reflects the content.

Credits

Amended Sept. 8, 2011, effective Jan. 1, 2012.

Editors' Notes

COMMENT TO 2012 AMENDMENT

The language of Rule 1008 has been amended to conform to the federal restyling of the Evidence Rules to make them more easily understood and to make style and terminology consistent throughout the rules. These changes are intended to be stylistic only. There is no intent to change any result in any ruling on evidence admissibility.

HISTORICAL NOTE

Source:

Federal Rules of Evidence, Rule 1008.

17A Pt. 1 A. R. S. Rules of Evid., Rule 1008, AZ ST REV Rule 1008

Current with amendments received through 11/1/17

Made in the USA
San Bernardino, CA
23 August 2018